WITHDRAWN

Once Again,
La Fontaine

D1404198

Wesleyan Poetry

841.4
L 13 on

Once Again,
La Fontaine

Sixty More Fables

Translated by
Norman R. Shapiro

Illustrations by
David Schorr

Introduction by
John Hollander

Wesleyan University Press
Published by University Press of New England
Hanover and London

*Publication of this book has been aided by a grant from
the Thomas and Catharine McMahon Fund, of Wesleyan University,
established through the generosity of the late Joseph McMahon.*

*This book was designed and typeset by David Schorr.
It is typeset in ITC Carter and Cone Galliard, designed by Matthew Carter;
and
Emigré Base 12 Bold, designed by Zuzana Licko in 1995.*

This book is printed on acid-free paper.

University Press of New England, Hanover, New Hampshire 03755
© 2000 by Norman R. Shapiro
Illustrations © 2000 by David Schorr
All rights reserved
Printed in United States of America
9 8 7 6 5 4 3 2 1

Library of Congress Cataloging-in-Publication Data
La Fontaine, Jean de, 1621–1695.
[Fables. English & French. Selections]
Once again, La Fontaine : sixty more fables / translated by Norman R. Shapiro ;
illustrations by David Schorr ;
introduction by John Hollander.
p. cm. — (Wesleyan poetry)
ISBN 0–8195–6457–5 (cloth) — ISBN 0–8195–6458–3 (paper)
1. Fables, French—Translations into English.
1. Shapiro, Norman R.
II. Schorr, David. III. Title. IV. Series.
PQ1811.E3 S45 2000
00–011730
841'.4– dc 21

In loving memory of
Lillian Bulwa,
who raised friendship to an art form
N.R.S.

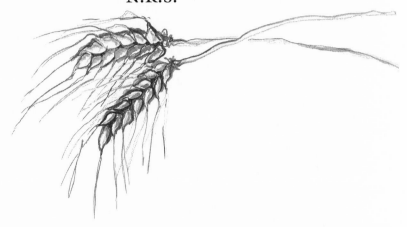

Some more pictures for
Arthur Williams,
who has no need of them
D.S.

ALLEGHENY COLLEGE LIBRARY

Contents

Translator's Foreword   xiii

Illustrator's Foreword   xv

Introduction   xix

L'Hirondelle et les Petits Oyseaux   2

The Swallow and the Little Birds   3

La Mort et le Mal-heureux, & La Mort et le Buscheron   6

Death and the Wretched Man, & Death and the Woodsman   7

Les Frelons et les Mouches à Miel   10

The Hornets and the Honeybees   11

Conseil Tenu par les Rats   14

The Rats in Council Assembled   15

L'Asne Chargé d'Éponges et l'Asne Chargé de Sel   18

The Ass with a Load of Sponges and the Ass with a Load of Salt   19

L'Astrologue Qui Se Laisse Tomber dans un Puits   22

The Astrologer Who Happens to Fall into a Well   23

Le Lièvre et les Grenouilles   26

The Hare and the Frogs   27

Le Lion et l'Asne Chassant   28

The Lion and the Ass Out Hunting   29

L'Yvrogne et Sa Femme   30

The Drunkard and His Wife   31

Les Loups et les Brebis   32

The Wolves and the Ewes   33

Philomèle et Progné 34
Philomela and Procne 35

La Femme Noyée 36
The Drowned Wife 37

La Belette Entrée dans un Grenier 40
The Weasel in the Larder 41

Le Berger et la Mer 42
The Shepherd and the Sea 43

La Moûche et la Fourmy 44
The Fly and the Ant 45

Le Jardinier et Son Seigneur 48
The Gardener and His Lord 49

L'Asne et le Petit Chien 54
The Ass and the Pup 55

Le Combat des Rats et des Belettes 56
The War Between the Rats and the Weasels 57

Le Cheval S'Estant Voulu Vanger du Cerf 60
The Horse Who Sought Revenge on the Stag 61

Le Renard et le Buste 62
The Fox and the Bust 63

L'Oracle et l'Impie 64
The Oracle and the Infidel 65

L'Œil du Maistre 66
The Master's Eye 67

L'Alouette et Ses Petits, avec le Maistre d'un Champ 70
The Lark, Her Little Ones, and the Farmer Who Owns the Field 71

Les Oreilles du Lievre   **76**
The Hare and His Ears   **77**

La Vieille et les Deux Servantes   **78**
The Old Woman and the Two Servants   **79**

Le Satyre et le Passant   **80**
The Satyr and the Passerby   **81**

Le Cheval et le Loup   **84**
The Horse and the Wolf   **85**

Le Laboureur et Ses Enfans   **88**
The Ploughman and His Sons   **89**

La Fortune et le Jeune Enfant   **90**
Dame Fortune and the Child   **91**

Le Lièvre et la Perdrix   **92**
The Hare and the Partridge   **93**

L'Aigle et le Hibou   **94**
The Eagle and the Owl   **95**

Le Pâtre et le Lion, & Le Lion et le Chasseur   **98**
The Shepherd and the Lion, & The Lion and the Hunter   **99**

Phœbus et Borée   **102**
Phœbus and Boreas   **103**

Le Cochet, le Chat, et le Souriceau   **106**
The Cockerel, the Cat, and the Little Mouse   **107**

Le Chartier Embourbé   **110**
The Wagoner Stuck in the Mud   **111**

Le Charlatan   **114**
The Charlatan   **115**

Les Souhaits   **118**
The Wishes   **119**

La Cour du Lion   **122**
King Lion's Court   **123**

L'Homme Qui Court Apres la Fortune, et l'Homme Qui L'Attend dans Son Lit   **126**
The Man Who Runs After Fortune, and the Man Who Waits for Her in His Bed   **127**

Le Chat, la Belette, et le Petit Lapin   **134**
The Cat, the Weasel, and the Little Rabbit   **135**

Le Savetier et le Financier   **138**
The Cobbler and the Financier   **139**

Les Femmes et le Secret   **142**
Women and Secrets   **143**

Le Rieur et les Poissons   **146**
The Joker and the Fish   **147**

Le Rat et l'Huitre   **148**
The Rat and the Oyster   **149**

L'Asne et le Chien   **152**
The Ass and the Dog   **153**

Le Chat et le Rat   **156**
The Cat and the Rat   **157**

Les Deux Chiens et l'Asne Mort   **160**
The Two Dogs and the Dead Ass   **162**

L'Huitre et les Plaideurs   **164**
The Oyster and the Adversaries   **165**

Le Loup et le Chien Maigre   **166**
The Wolf and the Scrawny Dog   **167**

Rien de Trop   **168**
All in Moderation   **169**

Les Poissons et le Cormoran   **170**
The Fishes and the Cormorant   **171**

L'Araignée et l'Hirondelle   **174**
The Spider and the Swallow   **175**

Les Poissons et le Berger Qui Joue de la Flûte   **176**
The Fishes and the Shepherd Who Plays the Flute   **177**

Le Songe d'un Habitant du Mogol   **180**
The Dream of the Man from Mogol Land   **181**

Le Loup et le Renard   **184**
The Wolf and the Fox   **185**

Les Souris et le Chat-huant   **188**
The Mice and the Screech Owl   **189**

Du Thésauriseur et du Singe   **192**
The Treasure-Hoarder and the Ape   **293**

L'Aigle et la Pie   **196**
The Eagle and the Magpie   **197**

Le Singe   **198**
The Ape   **199**

Notes and Bibliography   **201**
Audio Compact Disc Contents   **218**

Translator's Foreword

An admirer of symmetry, I would no doubt have decided to translate only fifty of La Fontaine's fables for the present volume were it not for the difficulty of finding an appropriate title for it. My first collection, *Fifty Fables of La Fontaine,* stopped at that number. I hadn't intended a second at that time, but La Fontaine is, for me, an addiction; and, taking advantage of the tercentenary of his death, I was happy to have an excuse, in 1995, to do another fifty. Its title, *Fifty More Fables of La Fontaine,* was obvious enough not to pose a problem.

But when, still addicted, I found that I couldn't resist doing a third, the title was a concern from the beginning. What does one call a collection of fifty anything after, first, "fifty" and then "fifty more"? Several inappropriate, awkward, and commercially confusing possibilities presented themselves: *Fifty Still More Fables, Fifty More Fables Again, Yet Fifty More Fables…* My eventual solution was to say "symmetry be damned," and opt for a different title altogether. This had the added advantage of allowing me further to feed my addiction by raising the number here to sixty.

As with the two previous collections, the present one offers fables chosen from all of La Fontaine's twelve books. Readers will notice, I think, that many of the ones translated here are among his longer, more philosophical texts, less well-known to the general readership than the usual fare memorized by French school children for generations and frequently anthologized. Indeed, like most of his fables, they are not really for children at all, despite the avowed pedagogical intent of the earliest. No one with only a child's limited life experience can fully appreciate their moral messages, any more than a child, with limited literary exposure, can revel in the aesthetic of his individual, engaging poetic style.

Messages and style… Like every translator I attempt to be faithful to both; to transmit La Fontaine's subjects—plots, scenarios, call them what you will— and to do so in a verse and a manner that, without slavishly producing a line-for-line equivalent, brings across, in English, at least something of what characterizes him in French. To read La Fontaine in the original is a joy; to translate him is no less so. I hope that my readers will experience, in reading these translations, some of the joy that has gone into their preparation.

Henri Regnier's eleven-volume critical edition, *Œuvres de J. de la Fontaine* (rev. ed. [Paris: Hachette, 1883–92]), replete with copious annotations, has again served as the source of many of my notes. Once again also, I have chosen

Ferdinand Gohin's French text of the *Fables* as presented in the Association Guillaume Budé's two-volume edition, *Fables choisies mises en vers* (Paris: Société des Belles Lettres, 1934), which purports to be a faithful representation of the last edition corrected by La Fontaine himself. Readers familiar with more modern French will notice that I have again reproduced it with all its often disturbing vagaries and inconsistencies of 17th-century orthography and punctuation, taking the liberty of altering only a few probable misprints.

It is, as ever, a pleasure to acknowledge the many friends and colleagues—and even friendly colleagues—whose help and encouragement have gone into the preparation of the present volume.

The sure ear of Evelyn Singer Simha has, once again, proved an invaluable asset, as has her willingness to listen, and I thank her warmly for letting me impose frequently on her good nature. Caldwell Titcomb has, as usual, been an intelligent reader as well as an ever-ready and much appreciated research source. And C. Thomas Brown has provided a measure of editorial help that has greatly facilitated my efforts

My thanks, too, to Seymour O. Simches, an inspiration for many years; to the Kielys, Robert and Jana, and Vicki Macy, for the hospitality of Adams House, Harvard University, where most of these translations were written; to Elizabeth Dulany, aficionada of fable literature, for her generous interest; to Rosalind Eastaway, for frequent secretarial help; to Sylvia and Allan Kliman, for much moral support; to Rita Dempsey and Carla Chrisfield, for putting up with me beyond the call of duty; to Tom Radko and Suzanna Tamminen, of Wesleyan University Press, for their confidence; Matt Byrnie and Teresa Huang, go-betweens *par excellence*; and, of course, to the memory of my mother and the example of her spirited way with words.

A pair of "*merci*" as well to John Hollander, for his scholarly, yet graceful introduction, and to my talented colleague, David Schorr, whose elegantly graphic wit and style have again enlivened my work.

N.R.S.

Illustrator's Foreword

I first collaborated with Norman Shapiro on the anthology *The Fabulists French*, which spans nine centuries of fables. As I studied the history of illustrated fables I saw that from early 15th-century blockbooks (which preceded movable type!) to Gustave Doré's wood engravings in the 19th century, illustrators preferred the carved immediacy of wood. Wishing to go with tradition, I produced thirty woodcuts. This was my first real foray into the world of drawing animals, let alone animals with human characteristics. Though I drew initially in pencil, I turned to *sumi*, Japanese Brush Ink and East Asian brushes, first on paper, and then directly on the woodblock. This technique allowed me to "capture" these beasts, the texture of fur and feathers as well as their expressions and gestures. There were a few humans as well, but they seemed to learn their expression and movement from the animals, rather than the other way round.

When Shapiro asked me to take on *Fifty More Fables*, I looked back to my earlier work, and decided I preferred these *sumi* studies to the woodcuts, and finished the illustrations in this fluid medium. Also at this point I decided to take on the design of the book. Book production having abandoned hot type and paste-up, everything was done on-line. The printer would send me (by e-mail!) scans of my own drawings which I could drop into the computer document containing the type. Here I discovered that, working either in Photoshop or QuarkXpress, I could alter my own drawings. Had I been designing for another illustrator I wouldn't have dared, and would of course have been furious if some designer had taken such liberty with my work. But I was free to make any changes I wished. Aside from the functional alterations like fading the occasional passage which read underneath type, I found myself most often stretching or squashing as well as tilting these characters to accentuate the narrative, making the lion more imperious, the rabbit more craven.

I had also noticed a certain formal difficulty in designing a book with facing page translations of poetry where the original on the left page always faced the translation on the right. The page-spreads had a predictable symmetry, which became quickly boring. The illustrations, I reasoned, could inhabit the symmetrical white space. Fables usually consist of a basic agon or confrontation between two dissimilar characters: the cricket and the ant, the cormorant and the crayfish, the kangaroo and the cassowary. Their inherent asymmetry provided a counter rhythm to the bilateral formality! And, as any book designer will tell you, it is tricky to run an illustration across the gutter where the pages are bound; I merely used that gutter as the psychological "no-person's-land" across which these characters glared and contended.

Continuing that basic strategy in this volume, I widened the margins, and, taking a cue from the title, decided to be more playful with the type. The fables in this collection are often more complex, and I wanted to reflect that complexity in the illustrations. Some, like "The Astrologer Who Happens to Fall into a Well," use the margins from left page to right to represent one character pictured twice as he moves through time rather than two opponents facing-off in space. There are also more complex casts of characters, humans interacting with animals ("The Lark, Her Little Ones, and the Farmer Who Owns the Field"), or third parties complicating the basic duality, as in "The Gardener and His Lord" where the point of view of the rabbit who begins the action confirms the foolishness of human behavior. And, finally, because fable writers traditionally "reinvent" each other's material—La Fontaine borrowed from Æsop, Sendebar, and others, while later writers borrowed from La Fontaine—I myself have adapted many images from the history of art and of illustration.

I must first of all thank Tom Radko at Wesleyan University Press for his faith in the Shapiro/Schorr collaboration method; in contracting a translation he undertakes a complexity of design, drawings and, in this case, soundtrack.

When Mary Ryan Gallery showed the drawings from the last La Fontaine and my prints from Shapiro's *Les Fleurs du mal*, an old friend, Douglas Sills, was the toast of Broadway as *The Scarlet Pimpernel*, but not too busy, given his infinitely generous spirit, to read from—perform really—both texts at my opening, to the delight of all. So when it was decided to produce an audio disc for this volume, Douglas seemed a natural to give voice to these characters. Once again I take advantage of his generosity. Arthur Williams and Mark Polycon of The Tape House, in New York City, provided a sound studio and Judith Weinstein directed.

To the staff at Wesleyan who help me in so many ways: Carol Kearney, Michele Ohlerud, Will McCarthy, Dan Schnaidt, and Lori Sikorski, I am forever grateful, as well as to Pam Tatge, the director of the Center for the Arts, and Stephanie Wiles, curator of the Davison Art Center. My dean, Diana Sorensen, and my Department Chair, Joseph Siry, were particularly supportive. To the Faculty and Administration and students of the National Institute of Design in Ahmedabad, India, where I began to work on this project, and to the Fulbright organizations in Washington and New Delhi, who sent me there, I am deeply grateful, as well as to the Administration and trustees of Wesleyan who so generously support sabbatical time for their faculty.

There are many friends and colleagues in the academic and artistic communities where I work, here and in India, who help me in ways general and specific: Walker Schiff, Clay Schiff, Jeffrey Schiff, Blair Tate, Noah Isenberg, Gay Smith, Gabriele Schnitzenbaumer, Vikas and Suranjana Satwalekar, Nina Sabnani, Aditi Ranjan, Vishesh Verma, Prashant Miranda, Rajni Nair, Sasi Gopal, Girish Shahane, Phyllis Rose, Laurent de Brunhoff, Nona Hershey, Andy Szegedy-Maszak, Jacqueline Gourevitch, Mark Koplik, Mark and Natalie Schorr, Wheelock Whitney, and the late Ranjabati Sircar—to all of you my thanks.

Mary and Cathy Ryan waited, with only mild irritation, for me to finish ("what? not another book!") so I could return to the paintings and prints I had begun in India. Doctors Richard Kaufman and Geoffrey Chupp kept the body alive through particular travail.

Cope Cumpston at University of Illinois Press had worked so closely with me on *Fifty More Fables* that this time I knew what I was doing. or thought so. John Elmore, once a student of mine, now a fine designer, is endlessly helpful with the twists and turns of Photoshop and Quark. Mike Burton at UPNE was infinitely patient with my graphic quirks. Amy Bernstein is not only a fluent designer and a computer whiz, she would rather help a friend than do something for herself. Without her, large projects like this and details of daily life would be endlessly more difficult, and certainly less fun.

In acknowledging my collaborator I will repeat what I said in our recent version of *Les Fleurs du mal*, made more appropriate here by the "topsy-turvy" world of La Fontaine: There is no way I can find words in any language, original or translated, to acknowledge Norman Shapiro, whom I now refer to as Gilbert, to my Sullivan—always with the reminder that Gilbert was the real genius.

D.S.

Introduction

The celebrated fables of La Fontaine perform a remarkably original turn on a remarkably fruitful tradition. Anecdotal stories of animals, endowed with human speech and who therewith represent human qualities, go back as far as Hesiod and Archilochus in early Greek poetry. We commonly associate such tales with the name of Æsop, a slave probably living on Samos in the sixth century B.C., and "Æsop" comes to designate the canonical author of fables written down only later by others; to this degree, he is authorship much like "Homer" or "Moses" or "David." The Greek word for "fable" (from Latin *fabula*) is simply "mythos," which means "story." (What we generally speak of as Greek mythology refers to the cycles of stories about gods and heroes.) A late Greek rhetorician, Theon, defined a fable as "a false story picturing the truth," but that "story" could be anything from a telling metaphor to a long and complex narration. The Æsopian stories, whether strictly of animals, or indeed, other sorts of parable, were in prose. But it was apparently an early practice to versify them. Plato tells us in the *Phædo* of how Socrates in prison, awaiting the execution of his sentence, took some fables of Æsop that he knew and turned them into verse, following the intimations of a dream to compose something. (He went beyond that in writing an Æsopian fable of his own.)

And so it is not surprising that some of the earliest Æsopian fables that we have are in verse. Horace, for example, has a speaker in one of his satires tell the familiar story of the country mouse and the city mouse; and versified collections in Latin by Phædrus, in the early first century A.D., and, slightly later, in Greek by Babrius were themselves imitated and paraphrased in prose and verse, and known in various collections through the Middle Ages. Chaucer tells and retells fables, and an elaborate version of one of them, in

"The Nun's Priest's Tale," is one of the world's great masterpieces of profound comic vision. Renaissance poetry contains many fables derived from Æsop, whether specifically of the animal sort or not. And fables in Sidney, Spenser, and Shakespeare lead to the spread of fable—often with a political agenda, as Annabel Patterson has shown—in the seventeenth century and thence to the extended and well-known fables of John Gay. William Cowper, at the beginning of a fable of his own, reminds us of the common Latin root of "fable" and "confabulate," and thereby of how much the matters of the animals talking is central to the form. He is also clear about the Æsopian world of a particular kind of fictive domain, by taking a passing swipe at Rousseau, who had insisted that no children be allowed to hear beast fables, since they were only vehicles of deception (animals *don't* talk and reason!):

> *I shall not ask Jean-Jacques Rousseau*
> *If birds confabulate or no.*
> *'Tis clear, that they were always able*
> *To hold discourse, at least in fable;*
> *And e'en a child who knows no better*
> *Than to interpret, by the letter,*
> *A story of a cock and bull,*
> *Must have a most uncommon skull…*

The Æsopian tradition gives frequent rise not only to new and later fables, but also to a certain amount of meta-fabling, of fables manifestly or implicitly about the mythopoetic bases of beast fable itself. In a fable in Sir Philip Sidney's romance *Arcadia*, for example, all the beasts ask Jove for a king to rule over them. He agrees but gives the yet incomplete human creature nothing but life itself, demanding that each of the animals contribute something of its own particular Nature: "The fox gave craft; the dog gave flattery; / Ass, patience; the mole, a working thought; / Eagle, high look; wolf, secret cruelty…"—a strange list, mixing zoological plausibility, cliché, and off-the-wall ascription.

English fabulists in the eighteenth century welcomed the beast-fable genre into their repertory of poetic genres, but they almost invariably condemned them to speak in one mode of verse only, rhymed tetrameter couplets, as in Cowper's lines above, or in these from the anonymously rendered Æsopian tale of "The Cat and the Old Rat," telling of how

> [...the cat] gets upon a Shelf,
> And to a String he hangs himself
> By one foot, dangling with his Head
> Downward, as if he had been dead.
> The Rats all thought he had been taken
> At stealing Cheese, or gnawing Bacon;
> Perhaps he might have foul'd the Bed,
> Murdered a Bird, or that he had
> Committed any other Evil
> By instigation of the Devil
> Or his own more malicious Nature;
> For which they hang'd the wicked creature.

Contemporary with these lines, too, is the cautionary tale into which Matthew Prior revised the well-known fable from Æsop of the cat changed into a woman, itself turned by La Fontaine into "*La Chatte métamorphosée en Femme*":

> *To My Lord Buckhurst, Very Young, Playing with a Cat*

> The am'rous youth whose tender breast
> Was by his darling cat possesst,
> Obtain'd of Venus his desire,
> Howe'er irregular his fire:
> Nature the pow'r of love obey'd:
> The cat becoming a blushing maid;
> And, on the happy change, the boy
> Employ'd his wonder, and his joy.

> Take care, O beauteous child, take care,
> Lest thou prefer so rash a pray'r:
> Nor vainly hope, the queen of love
> Will e'er thy fav'rite's charms improve.
> O quickly from her shrine retreat;

Or tremble for thy darling's fate.
The queen of love, who soon will see
Her own Adonis live in thee,
Will lightly her first loss deplore,
Will easily forgive the boar:
Her eyes with tears no more will flow;
With jealous rage her breast will glow;
And on her tabby rival's face
She deep will mark the new disgrace.

In France, versified Æsopian fables have a rich and interesting history as well, seeming to outlast the life of the mode in English (although Emerson's fable of the mountain and the squirrel is certainly squarely in the tradition). Professor Shapiro has himself previously translated a lot of these into English verse with the same kind of skill that he has brought to the Englishing of La Fontaine, commenting profusely and most enlighteningly on the French fable and its history.

The Greek myths in the Hellenistic handbooks were transformed, juxtaposed, intertwined and brought to an amazing life of meaning and feeling by the poetry of Ovid. In the case of the Æsopian fables, the great transformation was wrought by Jean de La Fontaine in the seventeenth century, who made the language of his fabulous creatures the material for his own remarkable poetic skill, controlling tone; using the original rhythm and pacing of the lengths of his lines and the placement of his rhymes; and deploying a kind of wit that often seems to be implicitly acknowledging that these creatures couldn't speak except in remarkable verse like this. His great collection of 250 fables in twelve books was published in three parts: the first six books in 1668, five more ten years later, and a twelfth volume in 1694, the year before he died. This rounded out an epical enterprise (there were twelve books in Virgil's Æneid) that is half signalled in the opening line of La Fontaine's dedicatory poem the Dauphin: *"Je chante les héros dont Esope est le père"*—"I sing the heroes whose father is Æsop". (La Fontaine's gifts as a neo-classical poet are apparent in his lovely poem *Adonis*, about which

Paul Valéry wrote a fine and central essay; he also invented the intriguing form of the *rondeau redoublé*, a mode which spins refrains out of its first quatrain.)

La Fontaine's collection contains fables of a variety of types drawn from a variety of sources (including those of the Indian fabulist Bidpai). The ones most familiar to English-speaking readers are perhaps those of the animal fables most often retold in other forms, or which became proverbial (the "sour grapes" of "*Le Renard et les Raisins*," the fox and the grapes), or which, when most educated people learned French, used to be memorized at school (*Maître Corbeau, sur un arbre perché, / Tenait en son bec un fromage*, etc.) But there are many other sorts as well: ætiological fables like the one Socrates proposed about pleasure and pain ("L'Amour et la Folie" is a splendid one of these), or poems of wittily revisionary mythography, like the one on what happened to the Goddess Discord after the Homeric fable got through with her, which are rooted in the traditions of Renaissance poetry. Stories of that sort contain their own moralizations, and most need no "application," as a concluding "moral" or interpretation was called in medieval story-telling.

But it is in the beast-fables that La Fontaine's moral and poetic thought interfuse in another way. We cannot be sure, when we hear a story about an ant and a grasshopper, for example, what is going to be talked about: could it be a fable of the Imagination, the grasshopper taking great leaps as a sort of insect Pegasus, while the drudging life of the ant permits it to be conscious of nothing more in the world than its burden, its task, its duty? That would, at any rate, be the grasshopper's story (or if "*cigale*" is more accurately translated as "cicada," then it's more a matter of singing, or fiddling, than jumping). But that would be the grasshopper-view. It is with the prudence of the ant that the Æsopian tradition has always sided, and which has had the last word. It is only through the creatures' discourse—by means of the relation between the arguments they offer and their habits, natures, and interests in the matter at hand—that the moral is deployed. La Fontaine carries the matter further than prior fabulists had ever done, for discourse is the substance of his animal world. "Natural" characteristics (or rather, Æsopian, as opposed to zoologically defined ones) play a good part in La Fontaine's world—foxes are foxy, cats never come off as more than con-men, and so on.

But the fictional power of these fables derives from two paradoxically opposed elements; on the one hand, a kind of "realism" for which the poet is celebrated (his animals are variously peasants, bourgeois, nobility, rather than the emblematic or heraldic creatures) and, on the other hand, the mythical matter of there being any discourse at all. In the epilogue to Book II, the poet acknowledges the power of his own fiction by insisting, with a significant rhyme on "vers/univers" that unites two senses of "creation," that

> *Car tout parle dans l'univers;*
> *Il n'est rien qui n'ait son langage:*
> *Plus éloquents chez eux qu'ils ne sont dans mes vers,*
> *Si ceux que j'introduis me trouvent peu fidèle,*
> *Si mon œuvre n'est pas un assez bon modèle,*
> *J'ai du moins ouvert le chemin…*

[For everything speaks throughout creation—nothing is without language; if, more eloquent at home than in my lines, those I present find me less than true to them—if my work isn't a good enough model, I've at least opened up a way]

But by "nothing is without its language," he does not mean what a naturalist would, but rather, as a poet, that he can make them say anything believably, and thus make moral discourse itself believable. As one commentator (Francis Duke) has so well put it, "La Fontaine is exquisitely aware of the relation of the speech of animals to the metaphor of the animals as man, whose proudest attribute is speech with words." A modern schoolboy's joke is apposite here, in that it pointedly deconstructs just this one crucial aspect of the beast fable: it is the one about a horse and a cow engaged in contentious argument, until a little dog that had been listening in silence suddenly intrudes by pointing out where a resolution lay, at which point horse and cow, shocked, both say to each other at once, "Look! A talking dog!!!" That the animals talk so well, and so humanly, runs along in counterpoint to the general Circean moral of all fabling, that people have animal natures usually hidden by language, custom, society, etc. These two notions entwined together make for the basis of La Fontaine's poetic world; and whether in the language of dialogue among the creatures, in the wonderfully flexible modes of narration, or in the whole range of tones that he adopts in his prefaces or appended moral applications; frequently these have as much archness, plainness, high diction or casual wisdom as any of his animals, the "*acteurs de mon ouvrage*," as he calls them.

La Fontaine's morals are not easily classifiable. His stories can take Stoic or Epicurean positions in turn, and speak variously as it were for ants and grasshoppers. He is of the age of Molière rather than of Voltaire, and his pragmatic naturalism and (as directly expressed in the verse essay serving as epilogue to Book IX) strongly anti-Cartesian views are accompanied by a clearly manifested love both of narrative and of his own characters, creating themselves through spoken language rather than, for the most part, ætiological myth.

The third century A.D. Philostratus, in one of his *eikones* or descriptions of imaginary pictures, shows the fables gathering "around Æsop, being fond of him because he devotes himself to them … And Æsop, methinks, is weaving some fable; at any rate his smile and his eyes fixed on the ground indicate this." This looks like La Fontaine, with his eyes fixed on his page, and his ear attuned to the two harmonies of human speech in all its variety, and the immense resources of formal verse. This seems more appropriate as a visualization of the spirit of the fabulist than the fantastic labyrinth built at Versailles, in the smaller park, in 1677, which contained thirty-nine remarkable hydraulic statuary groups of Æsopian fables, in which jets spurted or spewed from the mouth of each animal in a representation of speech (the machinery for pumping enough water from the

Seine to operate these cost the equivalent of tens of millions of dollars). At the entrance to the labyrinth stood statues of Æsop and, of course, Cupid (as Ariadne, holding in *his* hand the ball of thread as a guide to the way out of the maze—most poets would want to create some other figure holding the guide through Cupid's maze).

But just as Renaissance poetry, viewing the ruins of antiquity, could claim of itself that "Not marble, nor the guilded monuments / Of princes, can outlive this powerful rhyme," so the world of fable could arise anew in a dense, complex, self-referential and magnificently spirited poetry, rather than frozen into unenduring stone (the labyrinth was destroyed in 1775), and sounding only of splashing water, which is always nonsense until poetry makes it mean something.

Wandering through La Fontaine's world of fable is not in the least like going through one of the Sun King's labyrinths, but more like a walk through an English, or natural, sort of garden. The poet's muse, "*aux bords d'une onde pure,*" propounds its profusion of sorts of story, shades of ironic coloring, nuances of diction, turns of allegorizing strategy, and types of moral stance. But in all these types of tale it is what happens to them when they are "*mises en vers*" by this great poet that unifies them. The very verse itself—the so-called "*vers libres,*" of rapidly shifting line-lengths and rhyming schemes (not to be confused with "*le vers libre,*" the unrhymed "free-verse" of Rimbaud and modernity)—creates a tone which could be unsatisfactorily characterized as "wry," "witty," "distanced"—all of which are true of it—but which does more than that. Both the zigzagging of the line lengths, and the unpredictabilities even of its mode of unpredictability (the very famous poem of the country rat and the city rat is so regular in its quatrains of unvaryingly alternating lines of eight and seven syllables, cross-rhymed *abab*, that it is still sung as a children's song to a repeated melody), have both general and local effect. So, too, the wonderfully flexible diction, with its pointed and elegantly self-conscious use of archaic words here and there, and its constant reminders that this world of fable is like nobody else's. Even the American school child who used to have to recite the line about the fox addressing the crow (and, of course, his cheese) in *à peu près ce langage* "in language [sort of? more or less? approximately?] like this" would get the kind of joke—in its self-reference to animal discourse, which is *à peu près ce langage*, the language of the particular poem.

Professor Norman Shapiro has previously translated two large selections from La Fontaine's fables into exquisite and appropriately nuanced English verse. In Shapiro's versions, there is always an assurance of metrical control, and a sharp aptness to his decisions about diction, so that when, for example, he makes an egregious emendation or substitution, it often rings true. I shall quote only one of those he has previously translated, preferring the somewhat startling adjustments he makes to the old familiar fable of the fox and the crow (even with the almost outrageous allusion at the very end) to something chaster but less neatly done. The sense of play in, and with, the translation is somehow an appropriate version of the poet's own:

> Perched on a treetop, Master Crow
>   Was clutching in his bill a cheese,
> When Master Fox, sniffing the fragrant breeze,
> Came by and, more or less, addressed him so:
>   "Good day to you, Your Ravenhood!
> How beautiful you are! How fine! How fair!
> Ah, truly, if your song could but compare
>   To all the rest, I'm sure you would
> Be dubbed the *rara avis* of the wood!"
> The crow, beside himself with joy and pride,
>   Begins to caw. He opens wide
>   His gawking beak; lets go the cheese; it
> Falls to the ground. The fox is there to seize it,
>   Saying: "You see? Be edified:
> Flatterers thrive on fools' credulity.
> The lesson's worth a cheese, don't you agree?"
>   The crow, shamefaced and flustered, swore—
>   Too late, however,: "Nevermore!"

This may be the single fable most familiar to American readers, and to play with it requires some bravura. "Your Ravenhood!" for good old "Monsieur du Corbeau" and "*rara avis*" for "*le phénix des hôtes de ces bois*" are a little surprising, but by the time second thoughts have let them pass, they have already worked. More interesting to me is the sequence ". . . His gawking beak; lets go the cheese; it / Falls to the ground. The fox is there to seize it," where the series of enjambed lines culminating in the half-stumbling "cheese; it" is followed across the line break by the falling of the cheese into another clause ending in the middle of a line. But the whole is elegantly saved, in a completed pentameter line, when the fox is there to seize not only the cheese but, we feel momentarily, the fragment of verse—the fox catching the cheese itself catches the falling half-line, in a move that is pleased with itself even as it gives pleasure.

Shapiro, as in his version of these lines, seems almost to feel viscerally the way in which the English pentameter always stands in for the alexandrine—it's the "official," canonical line—and he uses it in this passage, as elsewhere, appropriately. But in general, it is his ear for the English iambic verse which is so well-tuned that his lines have the sort of authority of their own that gives credence to his strategies of adaptation and adumbration. His diction, also, seems remarkably flexible in exactly the right way.

It has been suggested that Circe was the first satirist; she turned men into the animals they "really" were; she made Odysseus' sailors into pigs, and Odysseus himself, but for the intervention of Hermes, a fox, or so Hawthorne suggested. Thus she invented one mode in which moral indignation has operated ever since, distorting the physical representation of people and their commodities in order to render correctly their usually hidden moral nature. She also thereby first allowed for the art of the animal fabulist, and so was, in a sense, the Muse of Æsop. The sixteenth-century Florentine writer G. B. Gelli, following a lead left unfinished by Plutarch, wrote a series of ten dialogues between Ulysses and a number of the animals who had been transformed from humans. After Circe's power was nullified, they had the option of returning to human form again, but in these conversations, each of the animals discourses eloquently, reasonably, and sometimes learnedly, about why he or she prefers not to. Given that they retain the language in which they can present their arguments, we might imagine that their preference is not for the animal state over the human, but is in fact their desire to remain fabulous. La Fontaine clearly loved them for that, as we indeed love him for showing us how much he did.

John Hollander
Woodbridge, Connecticut

Once Again,
La Fontaine

L'Hirondelle et les Petits Oyseaux

Une Hirondelle en ses voyages
Avoit beaucoup appris. Quiconque a beaucoup veu
Peut avoir beaucoup retenu.
Celle-cy prévoyoit jusqu'aux moindres orages,
Et devant qu'ils fussent éclos
Les annonçoit aux Matelots.
Il arriva qu'au tems que le chanvre se seme
Elle vid un Manant en couvrir maints sillons:
Cecy ne me plaist pas, dit-elle aux Oysillons.
Je vous plains: Car pour moy, dans ce peril extrême,
Je sçauray m'éloigner, ou vivre en quelque coin.
Voyez-vous cette main qui par les airs chemine?
Un jour viendra, qui n'est pas loin,
Que ce qu'elle répand sera vôtre ruine.
De là naîtront engins à vous envelopper,
Et lacets pour vous attraper;
Enfin mainte et mainte machine
Qui causera dans la saison
Vostre mort ou vostre prison.
Gare la cage ou le chaudron.
C'est pourquoy, leur dit l'Hirondelle,
Mangez ce grain, et croyez-moy.
Les Oyseaux se moquerent d'elle:
Ils trouvoient aux champs trop dequoy.
Quand la cheneviere fut verte,

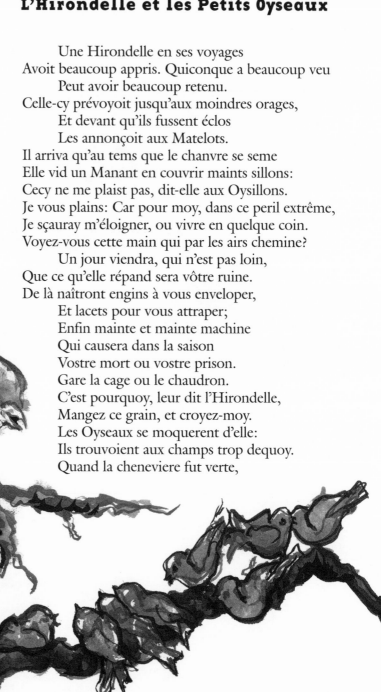

2

The Swallow and the Little Birds

A swallow, on her flights, had grown
Quite wordly-wise: surely when one has flown
    About and seen so many things,
It's going to follow that more than a few
Will one remember from those wanderings.
    This one, for instance, always knew
When storms—even the merest winds—would
And warned the sailors. Now, it happened that
She saw a farmer planting many a row
    Of hemp in season, and, thereat,
"Ah woe!" she mused, and promptly flew to tell
A flock of birdlings of the portent fell:
"You see that hand zigzagging in the air?
Soon will it deal your death, feed your despair!
The seeds men sow today they reap tomorrow.
And though each grain is harmless, they can be,
For such as us, the source of many a sorrow,
    Many a dire calamity,
    Though more for you, my pets, than me.
    Myself, I can fly off, or find
    Some nook protected from Man's kind,
    Safe from his lures, safe from his nets,
    And from his oh so many threats
    To life and limb—and wing! So mind
    You well, my pretties! You would not
    Conclude your days in cage or pot!
    Listen, then, when I tell you: Go

3

L'Hirondelle leur dit : Arrachez brin à brin
       Ce qu'a produit ce maudit grain,
       Ou soyez seurs de vôtre perte.
—Prophete de mal-heur, babillarde, dit-on,
       Le bel employ que tu nous donnes!
       Il nous faudroit mille personnes
       Pour éplucher tout ce canton.
       La chanvre estant tout-à-fait creuë,
L'Hirondelle ajoûta: Cecy ne va pas bien;
       Mauvaise graine est tost venuë.
Mais puisque jusqu'ici l'on ne m'a cruë en rien,
       Dés que vous verrez que la terre
       Sera couverte, et qu'à leurs bleds
       Les gens n'estant plus occupez
       Feront aux Oisillons la guerre;
       Quand regingletes et rezeaux
       Attraperont petits Oiseaux,
       Ne volez plus de place en place;
Demeurez au logis, ou changez de climat:
Imitez le Canard, la Gruë et la Becasse.
       Mais vous n'estes pas en estat
De passer comme nous les deserts et les ondes,
       Ny d'aller chercher d'autres mondes.
C'est pourquoy vous n'avez qu'un party qui soit seur:
C'est de vous renfermer aux trous de quelque mur.
       Les Oisillons, las de l'entendre,
Se mirent à jazer aussi confusément
Que faisoient les Troyens quand la pauvre Cassandre
       Ouvroit la bouche seulement.
       Il en prit aux uns comme aux autres:
Maint Oisillon se vit esclave retenu.
Nous n'écoutons d'instincts que ceux qui sont les nôtres,
Et ne croyons le mal que quand il est venu.

Feed on those seeds before they grow!"
So spoke the swallow. But the birds, each one,
Made fun, found her words hollow. "Ha!" they laughed,
"No need. The earth feeds well." And when the sun
Nourished the hemp to green, again they chaffed.
And when she cried: "Save yourselves! Pluck each stalk,
Each tender shoot that cursèd plant has sprouted!"
"Babbling old bird! Prophet of doom!" they shouted.
"Fine task you ask of us with all your talk!"
　　Enough of your absurd advice!
Even a thousand birds would scarce suffice
　　To try and strip the whole field bare!"
The swallow, when the crop had grown quite high,
Heavy with future evil, cast an eye
In its direction, adding: "Since you care
Little for all I've had to say till now,
　　At least beware, I pray, when men,
Putting aside their hoe, their spade, their plough,
Wage war on you with hempen snare. Best, then,
Either you never leave the nest, or move—
Like crane, and duck, and woodcock (and like me!).
But no. You're small, and it would ill behoove
The feeble likes of you to soar the sea,
The desert, seeking other climes. For you
　　There's really nothing else to do
But find some wall, some hole, and hide away!"
The birdlets, bored, chirp in their chitter-chatter:
Like Trojans lectured by Cassandra, they
　　Who heaped confused invective at her.
Birds, Trojans… Well, the former, like the latter,
Suffered in turn; for many, sore afflicted,
Lay trapped, ensnared, as swallow had predicted.
We heed no stranger's prophecies of woe,
And sneer at evil till it lays us low.

I, 8

La Mort et le Mal-heureux
&
La Mort et le Buscheron

Un Mal-heureux appelloit tous les jours
      La mort à son secours.
O mort, luy disoit-il, que tu me sembles belle!
Vien viste, vien finir ma fortune cruelle.
La mort crut, en venant, l'obliger en effet.
Elle frappe à sa porte, elle entre, elle se montre.
Que vois-je! cria-t-il, ostez-moy cet objet;
      Qu'il est hideux! que sa rencontre
      Me cause d'horreur et d'effroy!
N'approche pas, ô mort; retire-toy.

      Mecenas fut un galand homme:
Il a dit quelque part: Qu'on me rende impotent,
Cu de jatte, gouteux, manchot, pourveu qu'en somme
Je vive, c'est assez, je suis plus que content.
Ne vien jamais, ô mort, on t'en dit tout autant.

Ce sujet a esté traité d'une autre façon par Esope, comme la Fable suivante le fera voir. Je composay celle-cy pour une raison qui me contraignoit de rendre la chose ainsi generale. Mais quelqu'un me fit connoistre que j'eusse beaucoup mieux fait de suivre mon original, et que je laissois passer un des plus beaux traits qui fust dans Esope. Cela m'obligea d'y avoir recours. Nous ne sçaurions aller plus avant que les Anciens: ils ne nous ont laissé pour nostre part que la gloire de les bien suivre. Je joints toutefois ma Fable à celle d'Esope, non que la mienne le merite, mais à cause du mot de Mecenas que j'y fais entrer, et qui est si beau et si à propos que je n'ay pas cru le devoir omettre.

Death and the Wretched Man
&
Death and the Woodsman

Each day a poor wretch called on Death to come
    Save him from his cruel, wearisome
Condition: "Death," he would repeat, "how sweet you
    Seem! And how fair! Ah, I entreat you,
Come and deliver me from my fell fate!"
    Obliging, Death appeared, and thought
She would be welcome, since so much besought.
She knocked… Opened his door… Stepped in… But wait!
Shocked, the wretch shouts: "Horrors! Get rid of her!
Death, fearsome creature! Gruesome, sinister!…
    I want no part of you! Be off!"

It was Mæcenas [1]—something of a *philosophe*
    And fine *monsieur*—who, somewhere, said:
"Let me be dropsied, crippled, weak, bereft
    Of arm, of limb, with nothing left
But breath! Let me be anything, but dead!
    However helpless, feeble, spent,
Let me but live, and I shall live content."

This subject was treated differently by Æsop, as the follow-ing fable will show. Myself, I felt constrained to compose the preceding in order to give the subject, thereby, a more gen-eral application. But it was called to my attention that I might have done better to follow my model: that my version lost one of the most attractive features of Æsop's tale. Thus did I return to his. Never are we able to surpass the Ancients: they leave us only the glory of following them closely. I do, however, include my fable with his; not because mine deserves that honor, but because of the lines from Mæcenas that I repeat in it, so well-expressed and appro-priate to the subject that I thought it best not to omit them.

Un pauvre Bucheron tout couvert de ramée,
Sous le faix du fagot aussi-bien que des ans
Gemissant et courbé marchoit à pas pesans,
Et tâchoit de gagner sa chaumine enfumée.
Enfin, n'en pouvant plus d'effort et de douleur,
Il met bas son fagot, il songe à son malheur.
Quel plaisir a-t-il eu depuis qu'il est au monde?
En est-il un plus pauvre en la machine ronde?
Point de pain quelquefois, et jamais de repos.
Sa femme, ses enfans, les soldats, les imposts,
   Le creancier, et la corvée,
Luy font d'un mal-heureux la peinture achevée.
Il appelle la mort, elle vient sans tarder,
   Luy demande ce qu'il faut faire.
   C'est, dit-il, afin de m'aider
A recharger ce bois; tu ne tarderas guéres.
    Le trépas vient tout guérir;
    Mais ne bougeons d'où nous sommes.
    Plûtost souffrir que mourir,
    C'est la devise des hommes.

8

Bowed down beneath the weight of years, no less
Than by the burden of his heavy pack
Of sheaves—boughs, branches—bending low his back,
A woodsman, groaning, moaning his distress,
Goes trudging homeward toward his grime-smoked hut.
Weary, at length, of his travails and woe,
    Dropping his load, he muses: What
    Pleasure has he known here below?
Is there another who has suffered so,
Here on this mortal sphere? Sometimes, no crumb!
Nor any rest from all his laboring!
Wife, children, taxes, debts, toil for the king,
Soldiers to billet... Ah, the martyrdom! [2]
    And so he calls on Death to come,
Help him. She does, without delay. But when
    She asks what he would have her do,
"Madame," says he, "I merely called on you
To pray you help me lift my load again."
    Death cures our troubles by and by.
    Why hurry? Best we wait till then.
    "Better to suffer than to die."
    To which all mankind says amen.

I, 15, 16

9

Les Frelons et les Mouches à Miel

A l'œuvre on connoist l'Artisan.
Quelques rayons de miel sans maistre se trouverent,
    Des Frelons les reclamerent.
    Des Abeilles s'opposant,
Devant certaine Guespe on traduisit la cause.
Il estoit mal-aisé de decider la chose.
Les témoins déposoient qu'autour de ces rayons
Des animaux aîlez, bourdonnans, un peu longs,
De couleur fort tannée, et tels que les Abeilles,
Avoient long-temps paru. Mais quoy! dans les Frelons
    Ces enseignes estoient pareilles.
La Guespe, ne sçachant que dire à ces raisons,
Fit enqueste nouvelle, et pour plus de lumiere,
    Entendit une fourmilliere.
    Le point n'en pût estre éclaircy.
    De grace, à quoy bon tout cecy?
    Dit une Abeille fort prudente,
Depuis tantost six mois que la cause est pendante,
    Nous voicy comme aux premiers jours.
    Pendant cela le miel se gaste.
Il est temps desormais que le Juge se haste:
    N'a-t-il point assez leché l'Ours?
Sans tant de contredits, et d'interlocutoires,
    Et de fatras, et de grimoires,
    Travaillons, les Frelons et nous:

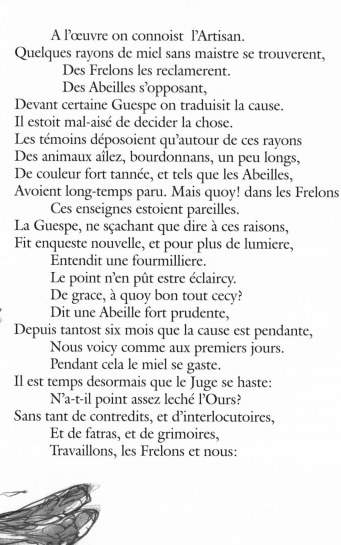
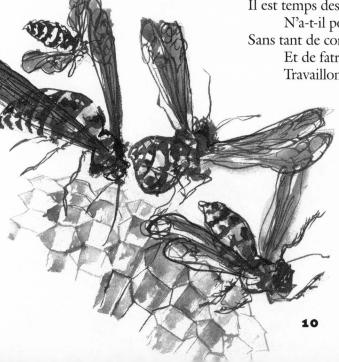

The Hornets and the Honeybees

"We know the workman by his work." [1] Quite so.
    One day some honeycombs were found,
    Abandoned. Hornets soon came round,
Claimed they were theirs. Bees challenged them: "No, no!"
Whereat a litigation was begun.
A wasp was chosen to decide between
The litigants. Easier said than done!
Witnesses testified that they had seen,
Buzzing about the combs, some wingèd creatures,
    Longish, tan-hued. "Like bees, I mean…"
    Aha!… But wait! Such are the features
Common to hornets too. The judge, perplexed,
With no idea at all what to do next,
Proceeds to call another trial; invites
    The ants to come and lend their lights
    In the affair. Useless endeavor!
Clearly the matter still remains… unclear.
    "Humbug!" protests a bee, more clever,
    Patently, than the rest. "Look here,
    Six months of chatter, and I fear
We're no whit closer than we were! I never
Saw such a twit! [2] Our judge will natter on
    And on, forevermore, with all
His legal tra-la-la and folderol.
    Meanwhile the honey spoils. Upon
My word, let's set to work, hornets and us:
We'll see whose toil produces sweet results."

On verra qui sçait faire avec un suc si doux
    Des cellules si bien basties.
    Le refus des Frelons fit voir
    Que cet art passoit leur sçavoir,
Et la Guespe adjugea le miel à leurs parties.
Plust à Dieu qu'on reglast ainsi tous les procez!
Que des Turcs en cela l'on suivist la methode!
Le simple sens commun nous tiendroit lieu de Code;
    Il ne faudroit point tant de frais.
    Au lieu qu'on nous mange, on nous gruge,
    On nous mine par des longueurs;
On fait tant, à la fin, que l'huistre est pour le Juge,
    Les écailles pour les plaideurs.

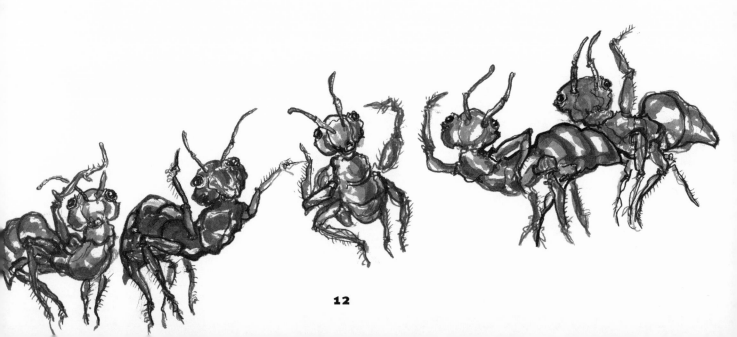

Hornets demur: theirs, no such skill. And thus
    His Honor cogitates, consults;
Sees their unwillingness as proof that they
Speak false; decrees the bees have won the day.
Good God! If only every case could be
Concluded with such speed, so easily!
Or if we followed, in our litigation,
    Methods known to the Turkish nation[3]—
Simple, direct! Then, I suspect, we might
    Duly dispense with *Lex* and *Jus:*
    Good common sense would rule aright.
    Instead we suffer law's abuse—
Expensive too!—till, in the end, so well
Do judges wear us down that, for their use,
They suck the oyster and leave us the shell. [4]

I, 21

THE HONORABLE

HYMEN
O.
PTERA

PRESIDING

13

Conseil Tenu par les Rats

Un chat nommé Rodilardus
Faisoit de Rats telle déconfiture
   Que l'on n'en voyoit presque plus,
Tant il en avoit mis dedans la sepulture.
Le peu qu'il en restoit, n'osant quitter son trou,
Ne trouvoit à manger que le quart de son sou;
Et Rodilard passoit, chez la gent miserable,
   Non pour un Chat, mais pour un Diable.
   Or un jour qu'au haut et au loin
   Le galand alla chercher femme,
Pendant tout le sabat qu'il fit avec sa Dame,
Le demeurant des Rats tint Chapitre en un coin
   Sur la necessité presente.
Dés l'abord leur Doyen, personne fort prudente,
Opina qu'il faloit, et plustost que plus tard,
Attacher un grelot au cou de Rodilard;
   Qu'ainsi, quand il iroit en guerre,
De sa marche avertis, ils s'enfuïroient sous terre;

14

The Rats in Council Assembled

A cat—one Nibblelard by name [1] —had spread
   Much misery and devastation
   Throughout the rodent population:
   Many a rat, alack, lay dead
And buried; whereas those still left—the few—
Daring not leave their hole in terror, grew
Hungrier by the day. Sire Nibblelard—
   He whom the people Rat, ill-starred,
Considered more a demon than a cat!—
Went whoring off one night; and while he plied
   His mate with amorous tit for tat,
   The remnants of his raticide
   Met in a corner and discussed
Their fate. "We have one hope! Just one!" So cried
   Their dean, indeed the most august,
   Most thoughtful of the lot. "We must
   Attach a bell, hang it about
   His neck, lest there be any doubt
When he comes out for war. Then shall we be

ALLEGHENY COLLEGE LIBRARY

Qu'il n'y sçavoit que ce moyen.
Chacun fut de l'avis de Monsieur le Doyen,
Chose ne leur parut à tous plus salutaire.
La difficulté fut d'attacher le grelot.
L'un dit: Je n'y vas point, je ne suis pas si sot;
L'autre: Je ne sçaurois. Si bien que sans rien faire
  On se quitta. J'ay maints Chapitres vûs,
  Qui pour neant se sont ainsi tenus:
Chapitres non de Rats, mais Chapitres de Moines,
  Voire Chapitres de Chanoines.

  Ne faut-il que deliberer,
  La Cour en Conseillers foisonne;
  Est-il besoin d'executer,
  L'on ne rencontre plus personne.

Able to flee!" They all agree:
    "Here, here! An excellent suggestion!
For more we cannot do!" The only question:
    Who? Who will bell the cat?[2] "Not me!"
Cries one. "I'm not so stupid!" "Nor am I,"
Assures another. Likewise all the rest.
And so they bid their brilliant plan good-bye,
As one by one they leave. Meeting recessed.
(Like many a conclave I have seen expire
For want of one brave canon, monk, or friar.)

    Advisers by the score abound
    At court to give advice. But set
    About to act, and you can bet
    There's no one anywhere around.

II, 2[3]

L'Asne Chargé d'Éponges, et l'Asne Chargé de Sel

Un Asnier, son Sceptre à la main,
Menoit en Empereur Romain
Deux Coursiers à longues oreilles.
L'un d'éponges chargé marchoit comme un Courier,
Et l'autre se faisant prier
Portoit, comme on dit, les bouteilles:
Sa charge estoit de sel. Nos gaillards pelerins,
Par monts, par vaux et par chemins,
Au gué d'une riviere à la fin arriverent,
Et fort empêchez se trouverent.
L'Asnier, qui tous les jours traversoit ce gué-là,
Sur l'Asne à l'éponge monta,
Chassant devant luy l'autre beste,

18

The Ass with a Load of Sponges, and the Ass with a Load of Salt

A donkey-driver, stick in hand—
    As if it were a scepter, and
Himself an august emperor of Rome,
    Though but a lowly muleteer—
    Was driving two beasts long of ear.
One, sure of hoof and trotting with aplomb,
Bore on his back a pack of sponges, while
    The other, dawdling donkey-style,
    "Crawling on eggshells," as they say,
    Was carrying a load of salt.
    Up hills, down valleys… Finally, they—
Staunch travelers—reach a stream, and there they halt.
The driver knows the spot; for, daily, he
Has forded there before. And so, upon
The sponge-packed ass he mounts, and urges on

Qui voulant en faire à sa teste
Dans un trou se precipita,
Revint sur l'eau, puis échapa:
Car au bout de quelques nagées
Tout son sel se fondit si bien
Que le Baudet ne sentit rien
Sur ses épaules soulagées.
Camarade Epongier prit exemple sur luy,
Comme un Mouton qui va dessus la foy d'autruy.
Voilà mon Asne à l'eau: jusqu'au col il se plonge,
Luy, le Conducteur et l'Eponge.
Tous trois beurent d'autant; l'Asnier et le Grison
Firent à l'éponge raison.
Celle-cy devint si pesante,
Et de tant d'eau s'emplit d'abord,
Que l'Asne succombant ne pût gagner le bord.
L'Asnier l'embrassoit dans l'attente
D'une prompte et certaine mort.
Quelqu'un vint au secours: qui ce fut, il n'importe;

C'est assez qu'on ait veu par là qu'il ne faut point
Agir chacun de mesme sorte.
J'en voulois venir à ce point.

The other beast, who, stubbornly,
    Doing just as he pleases (which
    Most asses do!), falls in a ditch,
Beneath the water. Thrashing for a bit,
He rises to the surface, but without
    A grain of salt! So well has it
Dissolved, that, now unburdened, can he flout
His master and go running off! The second,
Mimicking the example of his brother,
And like those sheep that follow one another, [1]
Jumps in as well. He hasn't rightly reckoned!
Not quite! For when up to his neck he plunges,
    Driver, and ass, and all the sponges
    Swallow their fill! Alas, the latter,
    Growing much fuller and much fatter—
    Heavier too!—weigh down our ass,
    Unable now to reach the shore.
Desperate our driver!… Well, it comes to pass,
As, clinging to the beast—behind, before—
He waits for certain death, that someone (who?
No matter!) saves both ass and driver too.

My moral here? That ill does it behoove
To follow, blindly, those ahead of you.
    That's really all I mean to prove.

II, 10

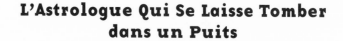

L'Astrologue Qui Se Laisse Tomber
dans un Puits

Un Astrologue un jour se laissa choir
Au fond d'un puits. On luy dit: Pauvre beste,
Tandis qu'à peine à tes pieds tu peux voir,
Penses-tu lire au-dessus de ta teste?

Cette avanture en soy, sans aller plus avant,
Peut servir de leçon à la pluspart des hommes.
Parmi ce que de gens sur la terre nous sommes,
    Il en est peu qui fort souvent
    Ne se plaisent d'entendre dire
Qu'au Livre du Destin les mortels peuvent lire.
Mais ce Livre qu'Homere et les siens ont chanté,
Qu'est-ce que le hazard parmi l'Antiquité,
    Et parmi nous la Providence?
    Or du hazard il n'est point de science.
    S'il en estoit, on auroit tort
De l'appeller hazard, ni fortune, ni sort,
    Toutes choses tres-incertaines.
    Quant aux volontez souveraines
De celuy qui fait tout, et rien qu'avec dessein,

The Astrologer Who Happens to Fall into a Well

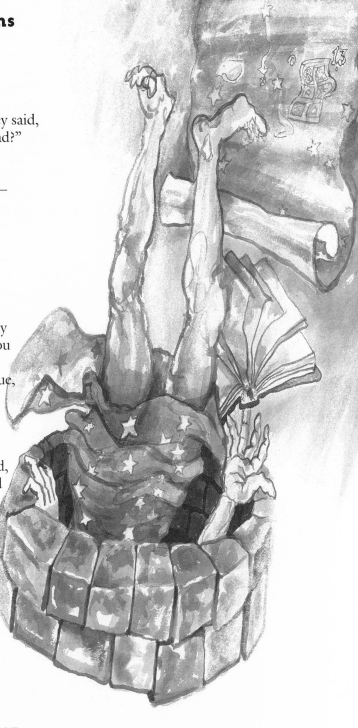

Once an astrologer there was, who fell
By accident, one day, into a well.
"Poor fool! If you can't mind your feet," they said,
"How can you read the stars above your head?"

Quite by itself, this misadventure can
Serve to teach humankind: many's the man—
    Or most—who can learn much thereby.
For who amongst us does not speculate
    With awe upon the Book of Fate,
    Sure of our power to plumb, descry
Therein our destiny! What was that book
    That Homer and his kind mistook
    For truth? How did the Ancients view
    What they called "chance," what we today
Term "providence"? Well, let me tell you, you
    Who think that chance's laws obey
Some science: nay, not so! For, were that true,
    We should not call it "chance," or "fate,"
    Or "fortune," all of which negate
    Science itself. As for the will
Of Him, the author of all good, all ill,
Who knows all, makes all, skillfully designed,
How can we comprehend, with feeble mind

Qui les sçait que luy seul? Comment lire en son sein?
Auroit-il imprimé sur le front des étoiles
Ce que la nuit des temps enferme dans ses voiles?
A quelle utilité? pour exercer l'esprit
De ceux qui de la Sphere et du Globe ont écrit?
Pour nous faire éviter des maux inévitables?
Nous rendre dans les biens de plaisirs incapables?
Et causant du dégoust pour ces biens prévenus,
Les convertir en maux devant qu'ils soient venus?
C'est erreur, ou plutost c'est crime de le croire.
Le Firmament se meut; les Astres font leur cours,
        Le Soleil nous luit tous les jours,
Tous les jours sa clarté succede à l'ombre noire,
Sans que nous en puissions autre chose inferer
Que la necessité de luire et d'éclairer,
D'amener les saisons, de meurir les semences,
De verser sur les corps certaines influences.
Du reste, en quoy répond au sort toujours divers
Ce train toujours égal dont marche l'Univers?
        Charlatans, faiseurs d'horoscope,
    Quittez les Cours des Princes de l'Europe,
Emmenez avec vous les souffleurs tout d'un temps.
Vous ne meritez pas plus de foy que ces gens.
Je m'emporte un peu trop; revenons à l'histoire
De ce Speculateur, qui fut contraint de boire.
Outre la vanité de son art mensonger,
C'est l'image de ceux qui baaillent aux chimeres,
        Cependant qu'ils sont en danger,
        Soit pour eux, soit pour leurs affaires.

Like ours, His mind's divine intent?
What? Has he printed on the firmament,
Stamped on the stars, what night veils from our eyes?
Why? For what purpose? So that they who write
About our earthly sphere might exercise
Their wit? Or so that we mere mortals might
　　Avoid the pitfalls lying ever
Ready to trap us? Or to make us lose
　　Faith in all joy, lest it abuse
　　Our senses; make us loathe whatever
Pleasures befall us, turning them to pain
Anticipated? Ah, how vile, how vain,
How evil such a thought! The heaven turns;
　　The stars follow their course; sun burns,
Brightens our days—perforce, day after night,
Night after day—for but the simplest reasons:
　　Bestow upon the earth his light,
　　Ripen her crops, bring round her seasons,
　　And keep our bodies well and fit.
As for Man's changing fate, how, tell me please,
Can changeless heaven do aught to alter it?
You charlatans, readers of destinies,
　　Begone! Quit Europe's royal courts,
You horoscoping idlers, and take with you
　　Those other quacks whose kin and kith you
Surely must be—those alchemists—retorts
And all!… Ah, but I rant. I mustn't. Back
　　Now to my tale about our quack,
Obliged to drink deep of the well: a model
Not only of practitioners of twaddle
But, too, of gaping moonbeam-chasers, those
Who can't see danger right before their nose.

II, 13

25

Le Lievre et les Grenouilles

Un Lievre en son giste songeoit,
(Car que faire en un giste, à moins que l'on ne songe?)
Dans un profond ennuy ce Lievre se plongeoit:
Cet animal est triste, et la crainte le ronge.
  Les gens de naturel peureux
  Sont, disoit-il, bien malheureux;
Ils ne sçauroient manger morceau qui leur profite.
Jamais un plaisir pur, toujours assauts divers:
Voilà comme je vis: cette crainte maudite
M'empesche de dormir, sinon les yeux ouverts.
Corrigez-vous, dira quelque sage cervelle.
  Et la peur se corrige-t-elle?
  Je croy mesme qu'en bonne foy
  Les hommes ont peur comme moy.
  Ainsi raisonnoit nostre Lievre,
  Et cependant faisoit le guet.
  Il estoit douteux, inquiet:
Un souffle, une ombre, un rien, tout luy donnoit la fiévre.
  Le melancolique animal,
  En rêvant à cette matiere,
Entend un leger bruit: ce luy fut un signal
  Pour s'enfuïr devers sa taniere.
Il s'en alla passer sur le bord d'un Estang.
Grenoüilles aussi-tost de sauter dans les ondes,
Grenoüilles de rentrer en leurs grottes profondes.
  Oh! dit-il, j'en fais faire autant
  Qu'on m'en fait faire! Ma presence
Effraye aussi les gens, je mets l'alarme au camp!
  Et d'où me vient cette vaillance?
Comment! des animaux qui tremblent devant moy!
  Je suis donc un foudre de guerre?
Il n'est, je le vois bien, si poltron sur la terre
Qui ne puisse trouver un plus poltron que soy.

The Hare and the Frogs

A hare, daydreaming near his lair
  (For, after all, what else is there
A hare can do when near a lair?)—distressed
  Beyond all measure, much depressed—
  Lay pondering and fraught with fright.
  "Poor fretful creatures we!" he mused,
  "Much to be pitied. Never a bite
  To eat in peace. Ever refused
  Life's simplest pleasure, never free
From fear! Damnable fear! Misery me!
  See? Even when I try to sleep,
  Can I? Oh no! I have to keep
  A watchful, ever open eye!
Many's the counsel—canny, wise, enlightened—
  Urging me not to run so frightened.
  Fiddlesticks! For, though hard we try,
Is fear so easy to be rid of? Why,
  I think that even humankind

Fears quite as much as I." And thus—resigned
To quake with fevered fright at just the slightest
  Shadow, the merest wheeze, the lightest
Breath that might breeze his way—the hare opined.
Soon, on his melancholic watch, he hears
A noise; not much of one, but to his ears
Such as to make him start; run, worrying,
Off to his hole, a-dart, Now, scurrying
Along a marsh, he sees, in unison,
  A clutch of frogs, each blessèd one,
  Flip and go diving, with a flash,
Into their grotto deeps, below. "Well, I'll
  Be dashed!" he peeps, amid the splash
And splutter; and, puffing his chest the while:
"What? Me, a terror too? My humble kind?"
And, now inclined to smile a little smile:
"However craven we, in heart and mind,
Creature more craven will we always find."[1]

Le Lion et l'Asne Chassant

Le Roy des animaux se mit un jour en teste
   De giboyer. Il celebroit sa feste.
Le gibier du Lion, ce ne sont pas moineaux,
Mais beaux et bons Sangliers, Daims et Cerfs bons et beaux.
     Pour réüssir dans cette affaire,
     Il se servit du ministere
     De l'Asne à la voix de Stentor.
L'Asne à Messer Lion fit office de Cor.
Le Lion le posta, le couvrit de ramée,
Luy commanda de braire, assuré qu'à ce son
Les moins intimidez füiroient de leur maison.
Leur troupe n'estoit pas encore accoûtumée
     A la tempeste de sa voix;
L'air en retentissoit d'un bruit épouvantable;
La frayeur saisissoit les hostes de ces bois.
Tous fuyoient, tous tomboient au piége inévitable
     Où les attendoit le Lion.
N'ay-je pas bien servy dans cette occasion?
Dit l'Asne, en se donnant tout l'honneur de la chasse.
 —Ouy, reprit le Lion, c'est bravement crié.
Si je ne connoissois ta personne et ta race,
     J'en serois moy-mesme effrayé.
L'Asne, s'il eût osé, se fût mis en colere,
Encor qu'on le raillast avec juste raison:
Car qui pourroit souffrir un Asne fanfaron?
     Ce n'est pas là leur caractere.

The Lion and the Ass Out Hunting

The king of beasts decided, one fine day—
Feting his birthday, so the story goes—
To hunt some prey. (We can, of course, suppose
   That he would not hunt sparrows, say,
Or such; but rather that he had in mind
Fine stag and deer, and boar of finest kind
As well!) And so, to help him trap his fare,
It was the ass who, as His Highness' choice—
   He of the brash, stentorian voice—
Would serve as trumpet with his brassy blare.
Concealed with bough and leaf, it was agreed
That he would bray and bellow. For, indeed,
Thus would those beasts who dared, though great their awe—
   Unused, as yet, to this hee-haw—
Come fleeing, each one from his lair or den.
   He did… They did… Alas! For when
The air resounded with his frightful sound,
Animals, taking to their hooves, all round,
Bounding and leaping, here, there, everywhere,
Found themselves, straightway, in the lion's snare.
"My talent won the day, *n'est-ce pas?*" "My ass,"
   The lion scoffed "naught can surpass
That bray of yours! Why, if I didn't know
What a crass twit you are, I would have been
   Terrified too!" Our ass, although
Deeply offended by King Lion's mot,
   Thought it was best, to save his skin,
   Simply to let the matter go.

II, 19

29

L'Yvrogne et Sa Femme

Chacun a son défaut où toûjours il revient:
      Honte ny peur n'y remedie.
    Sur ce propos, d'un conte il me souvient:
      Je ne dis rien que je n'appuye
   De quelque exemple. Un suppost de Bacchus
Alteroit sa santé, son esprit et sa bourse.
Telles gens n'ont pas fait la moitié de leur course
      Qu'ils sont au bout de leurs écus.
Un jour que celuy-cy plein du jus de la treille,
Avoit laissé ses sens au fond d'une bouteille.
Sa femme l'enferma dans un certain tombeau.
      Là les vapeurs du vin nouveau
Cuverent à loisir. A son réveil il treuve
L'attirail de la mort à l'entour de son corps:
      Un luminaire, un drap des morts.
Oh! dit-il, qu'est-cecy? Ma femme est-elle veuve?
Là-dessus son épouse, en habit d'Alecton,
Masquée et de sa voix contrefaisant le ton,
Vient au prétendu mort, approche de sa biere,
Luy presente un chaudeau propre pour Lucifer.
L'Epoux alors ne doute en aucune maniere
      Qu'il ne soit citoyen d'enfer.
Quelle personne es-tu? dit-il à ce phantosme.
     —La celeriere du Royaume
De Satan, reprit-elle; et je porte à manger
      A ceux qu'enclost la tombe noire.
      Le Mary repart sans songer:
      Tu ne leur portes point à boire?

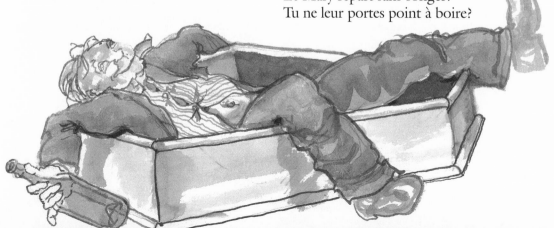

The Drunkard and His Wife [1]

Everyone has some vice that neither shame
Nor fear can stop him from returning to.
    I have a tale that shows how true
That is. (For never will I make a claim
    That I cannot support with ample
    Evidence from a good example!)
To wit: one of old Bacchus's elect,
    So much his devotee, had wrecked
    His health, his mind… And even worse,
    Had lost his wealth: empty of purse,
Such folk, before their race has been half-run,
    Haven't a blessèd sou. This one,
Full of the trellis-juice, one night, bereft
Of reason, thought, and consciousness, has left
His senses in the bottle. Thereupon,
His wife has him transported to a tomb
To sleep away wine's vapors. When, anon,
    He wakes, and sees the marks of doom
And death—the shroud, the candles funerary:
    "What's this?" he cries. "Is my wife now
A widow?" Whereupon said spouse, somehow
Changing her voice, masked, and in mortuary
Guise, Fury-like, [2] comes to the bier, presents
A stew fit for the devil's palate; whence
The drunkard knows that Hades now will be
    His home for all eternity.
He asks: "Who are you?" "Who? Who do you think?
Hell's scullery-nun! [3] I bring food for the doomed
To eat, here in the nether world entombed."
"Only to eat?" asks he. "Nothing to drink?"

III, 7

Les Loups et les Brebis

Aprés mille ans et plus de guerre declarée,
Les Loups firent la paix avecque les Brebis.
C'estoit apparemment le bien des deux partis:
Car, si les Loups mangeoient mainte beste égarée,
Les Bergers de leur peau se faisoient maints habits.
Jamais de liberté, ny pour les pasturages,
        Ni d'autre part pour les carnages.
Ils ne pouvoient jouïr qu'en tremblant de leurs biens.
La paix se conclud donc; on donne des ostages:
Les Loups leurs Louveteaux, et les Brebis leurs Chiens.
L'échange en estant fait aux formes ordinaires,
        Et reglé par des Commissaires,
Au bout de quelque temps que Messieurs les Louvats
Se virent Loups parfaits et friands de tuerie,
Ils vous prennent le temps que dans la Bergerie
        Messieurs les Bergers n'estoient pas,
Estranglent la moitié des Agneaux les plus gras,
Les emportent aux dents, dans les bois se retirent.
Ils avoient averti leurs gens secretement.
Les Chiens, qui, sur leur foy, reposoient seurement,
        Furent étranglez en dormant:
Cela fut si tost fait qu'à peine ils le sentirent.
Tout fut mis en morceaux; un seul n'en échapa.
        Nous pouvons conclure de là
Qu'il faut faire aux méchans guerre continuelle.
        La paix est fort bonne de soy,
        J'en conviens; mais de quoy sert-elle
        Aves des ennemis sans foy?

The Wolves and the Ewes

After a thousand years, and more,
The wolves decided they would end their war
Against the ewes: a wise decision
Both for the ones and for the others; for,
Although the former had a good provision
Of daily mutton (thanks to sheep that strayed
Far fom the flock), the shepherds often flayed
Said beasts to make their clothes. And so each side
Could neither graze with peace of mind
Nor kill its prey. Thus is the treaty signed;
Hostages are exchanged: the wolves provide
Their cubs; the ewes, their dogs—terms constituted,
Comme il faut, by commissioners deputed
There to officiate… Well, later on,
Those little cubs grew up, until,
Like proper wolves, hungering for the kill,
And waiting for the shepherds to be gone,
They seized the fattest, juiciest lambs, and snagged them,
Strangling them in their jaws, and dragged them
Off; whilst the dogs, no longer prone to keep
A watchful eye, lay slaughtered in their sleep
(By secret agents of the wolves!), so fast,
They didn't feel a thing: from first to last,
Each butchered by the wolves' foul villainy.
In which we can, I venture, see
A moral: peace is good; however,
Better yet is it that we never
Disarm against a faithless enemy.

III, 13

Philomèle at Progné

Autrefois Progné l'hirondelle
De sa demeure s'écarta,
Et loin des Villes s'emporta
Dans un Bois où chantoit la pauvre Philomele.
Ma sœur, luy dit Progné, comment vous portez-vous?
Voicy tantost mille ans que l'on ne vous a vuë:
Je ne me souviens point que vous soyez venuë
Depuis le temps de Thrace habiter parmy nous.
Dites-moy, que pensez-vous faire?
Ne quitterez-vous point ce sejour solitaire?
—Ah! reprit Philomele, en est-il de plus doux?
Progné luy repartit: Et quoy, cette musique
Pour ne chanter qu'aux animaux,
Tout au plus à quelque rustique?
Le desert est-il fait pour des talens si beaux?
Venez faire aux citez éclater leurs merveilles.
Aussi-bien, en voyant les bois,
Sans cesse il vous souvient que Terée autrefois
Parmi des demeures pareilles
Exerça sa fureur sur vos divins appas.
—Et c'est le souvenir d'un si cruel outrage
Qui fait, reprit sa sœur, que je ne vous suis pas.
En voyant les hommes, helas!
Il m'en souvient bien davantage.

Philomela and Procne [1]

Long years ago, the swallow—she, who in
    Her human form, before, had been
Procne, by name—went flying from her nest,
Far from the towns, into a wood wherein
Warbled the nightingale, and thus addressed
Her, who Philomela had been: "My dear!
Poor sister mine! How goes it? Many a year—
    A thousand? More?—has passed since we
Have seen you or enjoyed your company.
Since Thrace, in fact! So? Would you languish here,
    In solitude?" "What place more pleasant?"
Answers the nightingale. "What? Would you grace
Only the beasts with that uncommonplace
Music of yours? Or, at the most, some peasant?
Does wilderness deserve your gifts? Come, let them
Burst forth in cities, towns!… Besides, this wood
Recalls Tereus, your fair maidenhood,
And his foul, violent deeds! Best you forget them!"
"Quite!" says the nightingale. "And that is why
    I'll stay right where I am! For, when
    Any man, now, might greet my eye,
I live through that cruel horror yet again."

III, 15

La Femme Noyée

Je ne suis pas de ceux qui disent: Ce n'est rien:
    C'est une femme qui se noye.
Je dis que c'est beaucoup; et ce sexe vaut bien
Que nous le regrettions, puisqu'il fait nôtre joye.
Ce que j'avance icy n'est point hors de propos,
    Puisqu'il s'agit dans cette Fable
    D'une femme qui dans les flots
Avoit fini ses jours par un sort déplorable.
    Son Epoux en cherchoit le corps,
    Pour luy rendre en cette avanture
    Les honneurs de la sepulture.
    Il arriva que sur les bords
    Du fleuve auteur de sa disgrace
Des gens se promenoient, ignorans l'accident.
    Ce mary donc leur demandant
S'ils n'avoient de sa femme apperçu nulle trace:

The Drowned Wife

I'm not a man, like some, who, when they hear
"A woman's drowning!" scoff, turn a deaf ear,
　　And say: "So what? What does it matter?"
I say it matters greatly. For the tender
　　Sex (as they're called), the female gender,
　　Would be much missed. Without the latter,
　　Source of our joy, what would we do?
I speak of woman here neither to flatter
　　Nor to defend her, but, as you
Will see, because my fable tells the story,
Precisely, of a wife gone to her glory,
Alas, amid the waves. Her husband sought
　　To find her body, for he thought
It only proper, *a posteriori,*
To give it all the honors of the tomb.
Well now, it happened that some dawdlers whom
He spied, beside the stream, strolling about,
Near where she met her doom, were quite without
News of the fell event. He asked if they

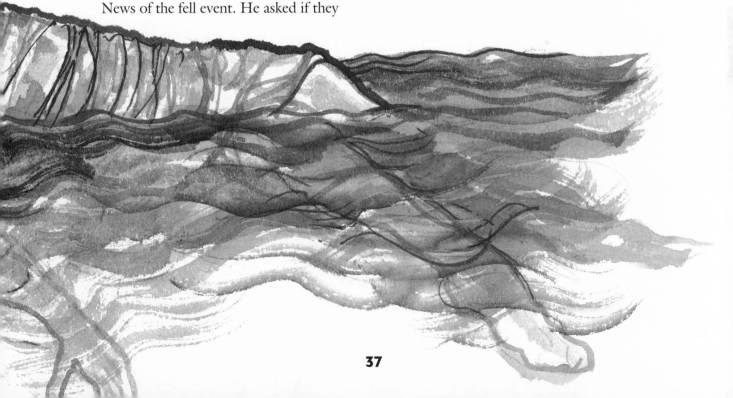

37

Nulle, reprit l'un d'eux; mais cherchez-la plus bas;
    Suivez le fil de la riviere.
Un autre repartit: Non, ne le suivez pas;
    Rebroussez plutost en arriere.
Quelle que soit la pente et l'inclination
    Dont l'eau par sa course l'emporte,
    L'esprit de contradiction
    L'aura fait floter d'autre sorte.
Cet homme se railloit assez hors de saison.
    Quant à l'humeur contredisante,
    Je ne sçay s'il avoit raison.
    Mais, que cette humeur soit, ou non,
    Le défaut du sexe et sa pente,
    Quiconque avec elle naistra
    Sans faute avec elle mourra,
    Et jusqu'au bout contredira
    Et, s'il peut, encor par-delà.

Had seen Madame float by. "Nay, nay,"
　　Was their reply. "But there's no doubt,"
Said one, "follow the river all the way:
You'll find her!" "Nay, not so," another said.
"Go back upstream, back to the watershed:
A wife, despite the current's predilection,
Surely would take the opposite direction!"
His wit was out of place, I must admit.
As for the gentle sex's tendency
To be perverse and contradictory,
I neither can deny nor vouch for it.
　　Let me say merely that if she
　　Is born to act contrariwise,
　　Contrariwise a woman will
　　Behave throughout her days, until
　　Her final breath, the day she dies:
　　Till death… And maybe longer still! [1]

III, 16

La Belette Entrée dans un Grenier

Damoiselle Belette, au corps long et floüet,
Entra dans un Grenier par un trou fort étroit.
     Elle sortoit de maladie.
     Là, vivant à discretion,
     La galande fit chere lie,
     Mangea, rongea, Dieu sçait la vie,
Et le lard qui perit en cette occasion.
     La voilà pour conclusion
     Grasse, mafluë, et rebondie.
Au bout de la semaine ayant disné son sou,
Elle entend quelque bruit, veut sortir par le trou,
Ne peut plus repasser, et croit s'estre méprise.
     Aprés avoir fait quelques tours:
C'est, dit-elle, l'endroit, me voilà bien surprise;
J'ay passé par icy depuis cinq ou six jours.
     Un Rat qui la voyoit en peine
Luy dit: Vous aviez lors la panse un peu moins pleine.
Vous estes maigre entrée, il faut maigre sortir.
Ce que je vous dis là, l'on le dit à bien d'autres.
Mais ne confondons point, par trop approfondir,
     Leurs affaires avec les vostres.

The Weasel in the Larder

Weasel—that lissome-bodied *demoiselle*—
Risen from sickbed, though not yet quite well
   (Indeed, grown wan and slightly withered),
Finding a hole of very small dimension,
   Into a larder lithely slithered,
   Sprightly, and with the firm intention
   There to remain midst all that glut.
And so remain she did, gorging her fill,
Blithely gnawing her wanton way, until—
God knows!—no gammon lay unscathed. Ah, but
Now what a change in her avoirdupois!
   Fat, plump of cheek, bloated of gut
(All in one week!), at length she hears a noise,
Hurries back to her hole… Squeezes… "Oh oh!"
   She squeals, and scurrying here, there,
Thinks that, perhaps, she errs. "No! I declare,
It's the same hole! The one, a week ago,
I entered through!" A rat who witnessed her
   Chagrin piped up: "Last week, *ma sœur*,
Your belly wasn't quite so full! For, thin
   You were, and sleek, when you came in;
   Thin must you be when you go out."
And we concur: there's much to learn therein.
(But don't infer it's you my tale's about!)

III, 17

Le Berger et la Mer

Du rapport d'un troupeau dont il vivoit sans soins
Se contenta long-temps un voisin d'Amphitrite.
     Si sa fortune estoit petite,
     Elle estoit seure tout au moins.
A la fin les tresors déchargez sur la plage
Le tenterent si bien qu'il vendit son troupeau,
Trafiqua de l'argent, le mit entier sur l'eau;
     Cet argent perit par naufrage.
Son maistre fut reduit à garder les Brebis:
Non plus Berger en chef comme il estoit jadis,
Quand ses propres Moutons paissoient sur le rivage;
Celuy qui s'estoit veu Corydon ou Tircis
     Fut Pierrot, et rien davantage.
Au bout de quelque temps il fit quelques profits,
     Racheta des bestes à laine;
Et, comme un jour les vents retenant leur haleine
Laissoient paisiblement aborder les vaisseaux:
Vous voulez de l'argent, ô Mesdames les Eaux,
Dit-il, adressez-vous, je vous prie, à quelque-autre:
     Ma foy, vous n'aurez pas le nostre.

Cecy n'est pas un conte à plaisir inventé.
     Je me sers de la verité
     Pour montrer par experience
     Qu'un sou quand il est assuré
     Vaut mieux que cinq en esperance;
Qu'il se faut contenter de sa condition;
Qu'aux conseils de la Mer et de l'Ambition
     Nous devons fermer les oreilles.
Pour un qui s'en loüera, dix mille s'en plaindront.
     La Mer promet monts et merveilles;
Fiez-vous-y, les vents et les voleurs viendront.

The Shepherd and the Sea

A shepherd dwelt beside the mighty
    Sea—rich domain of Amphitrite,
Wife of Poseidon—amply satisfied
To earn the pittance that his sheep were worth,
    Secure, at least, despite his dearth
    Of worldly wealth. But soon the tide,
Strewing the shore with treasures of the earth,
From far and wide, tempted him, and he sold
His flock: lock, stock, and barrel; put his gold
Into the merchant trade, plying the deep.
A shipwreck gobbled down his fortune. Now,
Our would-be man of means, trying somehow
To earn his bread, turned once again to sheep;
Another's though—not like that time, long gone,
When, latterday Tircis and Corydon,
He owned the flock: now, humbly, mere Pierrot. [1]
In time he earned a little, bought a few
Sheep of his own: wool-laden lamb and ewe.
But when, one day, the winds, ceasing to blow
    Their gales, let ships approach the shore:
"No, Water-Wenches!" he exclaims. "No more!
You want my wealth? Well, fie on your design!
Try someone else, mesdames! You won't get mine!"

This is no idle tale I tell, indeed,
Invented but to please. Experience
Proves that a single sou, when guaranteed,
Buys more than five, promised some vague time hence!
Better to be contented with our lot
And not give ear to Ocean's tommyrot
    Or vain ambition's blandishments.
For each who tastes success, the fickle seas
Ruin ten thousand other devotees,
Condemned to wail their losses! Best beware
Lest tempests, thieves, make haste to seize their share!

IV, 2

43

La Moûche et la Fourmy

La Moûche et la Fourmy contestoient de leur prix.
    O Jupiter! dit la premiere,
Faut-il que l'amour propre aveugle les esprits
    D'une si terrible maniere,
    Qu'un vil et rampant animal
A la fille de l'air ose se dire égal?
Je hante les Palais; je m'assied à ta table:
Si l'on t'immole un bœuf, j'en goûte devant toy;
Pendant que celle-cy, chetive et miserable,
Vit trois jours d'un festu qu'elle a traîné chez soy.
    Mais, ma mignonne, dites-moy,
Vous campez-vous jamais sur la teste d'un Roy,
    D'un Empereur, ou d'une Belle?
Je le fais; et je baise un beau sein quand je veux:
    Je me joüe entre des cheveux;
Je rehausse d'un teint la blancheur naturelle;
Et la derniere main que met à sa beauté
    Une femme allant en conqueste,
C'est un ajustement des Moûches emprunté.
    Puis allez-moy rompre la teste
    De vos greniers. —Avez-vous dit?
    Luy repliqua la ménagere.
Vous hantez les Palais; mais on vous y maudit.

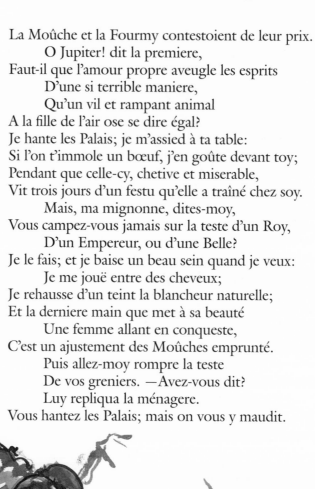
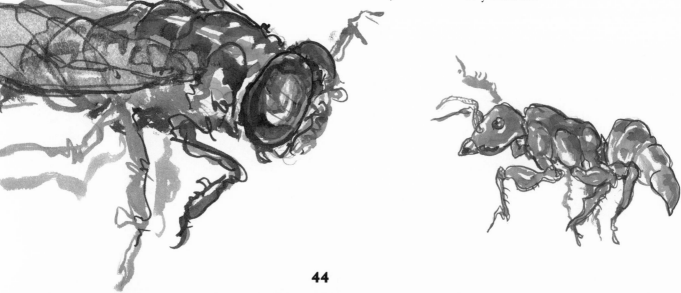

The Fly and the Ant

The fly and ant—a pair of insectkind's
Contentious foes—were vying: each one strove
   To prove the worthier. "O Jove,"
   Exclaimed the first, "see how our minds
Are blinded by our vanity! That crawling
   Beast dares compare herself to me!
Me, daughter of the air itself! Appalling!
My kind frequents fine palaces! Why, we
Even dine in your godly company:
For, when an ox or bull is slain, to do
You honor, I am there to taste it too,
Even before you, while my vain *consœur*
Lives for three days on but a wisp of grass
   That she goes dragging off to her
   Dark hole!… Tell me, my precious lass,
Can you light on an emperor's head, or on
   A king's, or on a beauteous belle's?
Well, I can! And if I should choose, anon,
I can plant kisses on a damosel's
   Fair breast! Or frolic in her hair!
And when she would impart a brighter air
To pallid tint, she adds a beauty spot—
   The one the French call "fly"—a dot [1]
Of blackest black… Now, after that, *ma chère*,
Go prattle on with all that tommyrot
About your precious larder!" "Are you through?"
   Queries the thrifty ant. "It's true,

Et quant à goûter la premiere
De ce qu'on sert devant les Dieux,
Croyez-vous qu'il en vaille mieux?
Si vous entrez par tout, aussi font les profanes.
Sur la teste des Rois et sur celle des Asnes
Vous allez vous planter; je n'en disconviens pas;
Et je sçay que d'un prompt trépas
Cette importunité bien souvent est punie.
Certain ajustement, dites-vous, rend jolie.
J'en conviens: il est noir ainsi que vous et moy.
Je veux qu'il ait nom Moûche; est-ce un sujet pourquoy
Vous fassiez sonner vos merites?
Nomme-t-on pas aussi Moûches les parasites?
Cessez donc de tenir un langage si vain;
N'ayez plus ces hautes pensées:
Les Moûches de Cour sont chassées,
Les Moûcharts sont pendus; et vous mourrez de faim,
De froid, de langueur, de misere,
Quand Phœbus regnera sur un autre hemisphere.
Alors je joüiray du fruit de mes travaux.
Je n'iray par monts ny par vaux
M'exposer au vent, à la pluye.
Je vivray sans mélancolie.
Le soin que j'auray pris, de soin m'exemptera.
Je vous enseigneray par là
Ce que c'est qu'une fausse ou veritable gloire.
Adieu: je perds le temps: laissez-moy travailler.
Ny mon grenier ny mon armoire
Ne se remplit à babiller.

Frequent fine palaces, you do. But when
 You do, they curse you there! And when you
Nibble the gods' repasts, to test their menu,
Do you improve their taste? Now and again
 You squat on heads of emperors. So?
 You sit on ass heads too! And woe
Attends you oftener than not thereby!
As for that bagatelle, that dot, that little
Beauty spot... Yes, the French do call it "fly"—
Black, love, like you (though no more so than I!)—
But how does that name give the merest tittle,
The merest jot of cause to flit and buzz
 Your merits roundabout? No, coz,
Enough high-sounding talk and vile self-praise!
Flies, don't forget, are parasites; and courts
Abound with such, all tattling false reports,
Tales, lies, till exile—or the gibbet—pays
Those fly-folk for their parasitic ways!
 You and your kind will die, my dear—
Languish in hunger, misery, and cold—
When Phœbus lights the other hemisphere,
Soon, with his brilliant rays of summer gold.
Then will my labors bear their fruit. I'll not
 Go anguish over hill and plain,
 Buffeted by the winds, the rain:
Sorrow and sadness will not be my lot!
 My care and foresight, *au contraire,*
 Will save me from such woe and care;
 And by my deeds I'll show you what
True merit is! But babbling here with you,
Ma chère, won't fill my cupboards full. Adieu! [2]

IV, 3

47

Le Jardinier et Son Seigneur

Un amateur du jardinage,
Demy Bourgeois, demy manant,
Possedoit en certain Village
Un jardin assez propre, et le clos à tenant.
Il avoit de plant vif semé cette étenduë;
Là croissoit à plaisir l'oseille et la laituë,
Dequoy faire à Margot, pour sa feste, un bouquet;
Peu de jasmin d'Espagne, et force serpolet.
Cette felicité par un Lievre troublée
Fit qu'au Seigneur du Bourg nostre homme se plaignit.
Ce maudit animal vient prendre sa goulée
Soir et matin, dit-il, et des pieges se rit:
Les pierres, les bastons y perdent leur credit.
Il est Sorcier, je croy. — Sorcier? je l'en défie,
Repartit le Seigneur. Fust-il diable, Miraut,
En dépit de ses tours, l'attrapera bien-tost.
Je vous en déferay, bon homme, sur ma vie.
— Et quand? — Et dés demain, sans tarder plus long-temps.
La partie ainsi faite, il vient avec ses gens:
Ça, déjeunons, dit-il; vos poulets sont-ils tendres?
La fille du logis, qu'on vous voye, approchez.
Quand la marierons-nous? quand aurons-nous des gendres?
Bon homme, c'est ce coup qu'il faut, vous m'entendez,
Qu'il faut foüiller à l'escarcelle.
Disant ces mots, il fait connoissance avec elle,
Auprés de luy la fait asseoir,
Prend une main, un bras, leve un coin de mouchoir;
Toutes sotises dont le Belle
Se défend avec grand respect;
Tant qu'au pere à la fin cela devient suspect.

The Gardener and His Lord

A certain villager—not quite
A burgher, nor a peasant—took delight
   In all of gardening's pleasures; and
   In fact, he owned a plot of land
   Next to a well-kept lot, whose edge
   Was bounded by a living hedge,
And in which grew, all round, thyme, salad, sorrel,
Some Spanish jasmine too… Ah, the bouquets
He made to fete young Margot's festive days
With living tribute, vegetal and floral!
Soon, though, this pleasant state of plant affairs
Was troubled by one of your hungrier hares!
Our friend goes to the village's *seigneur*,
Complains: "That damned beast comes and fills his belly—
Day, night, whenever!… Sticks? Stones? Traps? Too well he
Laughs at them all! No, he's a sorcerer,
I tell you!" "Well, you may well think so; still
Even were he the devil, friend, my hound
Miraut will run the nasty imp to ground,
I vow!" "Oh? How? And when?" "Tomorrow will
   I come." And come he did. Next day,
   True to his word, he and his men
   Arrive. "Now then, my friend, what say
   We eat? I trust you have a hen—
Or two, or three!—tender enough to be
A proper luncheon!… Ah! Who's that I see,
   Monsieur? Your daughter?… Come, my dear…
   Come here, my sweet, and sit by me!…
   Well now, is there no cavalier,
No beau who seeks the hand of this fair belle?
Methinks it's time we find some bagatelle

Cependant on fricasse, on se ruë en cuisine.
De quand sont vos jambons? Ils ont fort bonne mine.
—Monsieur, ils sont à vous.—Vraiment! dit le Seigneur;
	Je les reçois, et de bon cœur.
Il déjeûne tres bien, aussi fait sa famille,
Chiens, chevaux et valets, tous gens bien endentez:

Here in my purse for her!...[1] Dear child, come sit..."
    Whence he, with lustful little pat,
Fondles a hand, an arm, lifts up a bit
Of kerchief... With respectful tit for tat
    The wench resists, as would befit
A maiden... Soon her father grows suspicious;
And, as the spit turns, in the kitchen: "Oh!

Il commande chez l'hoste, y prend des libertez,
      Boit son vin, caresse sa fille.
L'embarras des Chasseurs succede au déjeuné.
      Chacun s'anime et se prépare:
Les trompes et les cors font un tel tintamarre,
      Que le bon homme est étonné.
Le pis fut que l'on mit en piteux équipage
Le pauvre potager; adieu planches, quarreaux;
      Adieu chicorée et poreaux;
      Adieu dequoy mettre au potage:
Le Lievre estoit gisté dessous un maistre chou.
On le queste, on le lance, il s'enfuit par un trou,
Non pas trou, mais troüée, horrible et large playe
      Que l'on fit à la pauvre haye
Par ordre du Seigneur: car il eust esté mal
Qu'on n'eust pû du jardin sortir tout à cheval.
Le bon homme disoit: Ce sont là jeux de Prince.
Mais on le laissoit dire; et les chiens et les gens
Firent plus de degât en une heure de temps
      Que n'en auroient fait en cent ans
      Tous les Lievres de la Province.

Petits Princes, vuidez vos debats entre vous:
De recourir aux Rois vous seriez de grands fous.
Il ne les faut jamais engager dans vos guerres,
      Ni les faire entrer sur vos terres.

What lovely hams! And fresh? They look delicious!"
"They're yours, *seigneur!*" "Too kind!… I'll take them though!…"
So goes the meal. He and his retinue—
His varlets, horses, hounds—swill down their fill,
Without so much as a *merci beaucoup!*
The lord, now master of the domicile,
Drinks Monsieur's wine, makes free with Mademoiselle,
And does, in short, what sport he will. Lunch done,
　　Comes time to hunt the hare. Each one—
A horde!—prepares. Horns, trumpets sound the knell
Of his poor garden! Ravaged, overrun,
Torn up, torn down, by that marauding troop!
　　Farewell leeks! Farewell chicory!
Adieu forever vegetable soup!
Our hare, the while, was hunching peaceably
Under a giant cabbage… "Tally-ho!"…
He scurries through a hole. A hole? Well, no,
Rather a gaping wound, a passageway
Slashed through the hedge so that His Lordship may
Dash through on horseback! "Why such princely sport?"
Queries the gardener. Still, they smash, cavort,
And wreak more havoc in one hour than all
The hares that flourished since the days of Gaul. [2]

　　You petty princes, caught up short
　　In wars! Fight them yourselves! For, more you
Lose when you let the king come fight them for you!

IV, 4

53

L'Asne et le Petit Chien

Ne forçons point nostre talent;
Nous ne ferions rien avec grace.
Jamais un lourdaut, quoy qu'il fasse,
Ne sçauroit passer pour galant.
Peu de gens que le Ciel cherit et gratifie
Ont le don d'agréer infus avec la vie.
C'est un point qu'il leur faut laisser,
Et ne pas ressembler à l'Asne de la Fable,
Qui, pour se rendre plus aimable
Et plus cher à son Maistre, alla le caresser.
Comment! disoit-il en son ame,
Ce Chien, parce qu'il est mignon,
Vivra de pair à compagnon
Avec Monsieur, avec Madame,
Et j'auray des coups de baston?
Que fait-il? Il donne la pate,
Puis aussi-tost il est baisé.
S'il en faut faire autant afin que l'on me flate,
Cela n'est pas bien mal-aisé.
Dans cette admirable pensée,
Voyant son Maistre en joye, il s'en vient lourdement,
Leve une corne toute usée,
La luy porte au menton fort amoureusement,
Non sans accompagner pour plus grand ornement
De son chant gracieux cette action hardie.
Oh oh! quelle caresse, et quelle melodie!
Dit le Maistre aussi-tost. Holà, Martin bâton.
Martin bâton accourt; l'Asne change de ton.
Ainsi finit la Comedie.

The Ass and the Pup

Folly it is to give the lie
To your true nature. Whence, infer:
A lout, however hard he try,
Never can be the fine *monsieur*.
Since but a precious few the heavens endow
    With power to please, best not allow
Yourself to do what, in my tale, a poor,
    Sorry ass did to court disaster.
Wanting to be more loving toward his master—
    More loved as well—the silly boor,
Flinging his hooves about his neck, caressed
    And kissed him, musing: "Just because
His pup's a dear, must he alone be blessed?
What does he do? He sits up, gives his paws,
Lives with Monsieur, Madame… Why, him they kiss
    And me they beat. Well now, if this
    Is all it takes, I vow, I'll do it."
So, seeing his master in a festive mood,
No sooner has he mused than he hops to it,
    In a most amorous attitude,
Clumsily pressing ragged horn to chin;
And, with his graceful song braying a din
To make his daring feat more charming yet!
Oh, that caress! That melody! Alarmed,
    Monsieur calls for his minions, armed
    With cudgels, sticks… "Help, help!…" They set
    Upon the ass, whose caterwauls
Change now from song of love to wail of woe,
    Beneath blow after blow… And so
        The curtain falls.

IV, 5

55

Le Combat des Rats
et des Belettes

La nation des Belettes,
Non plus que celle des Chats,
Ne veut aucun bien aux Rats;
Et sans les portes étretes
De leurs habitations,
L'animal à longue eschine
En feroit, je m'imagine,
De grandes destructions.
Or une certaine année
Qu'il en estoit à foison,
Leur Roy nommé Ratapon,
Mit en campagne une armée.
Les Belettes de leur part
Déployerent l'étendard.
Si l'on croit la Renommée,
La Victoire balança.
Plus d'un Gueret s'engraissa
Du sang de plus d'une bande.
Mais la perte la plus grande
Tomba presque en tous endroits
Sur le peuple Souriquois.

The War Between the Rats
and the Weasels

Like the people known as Cat,
Weasels have no great affection
For the nation of the Rat;
And, but for the cramped confection
Of the latter's entryways,
Many a weasel would, a-slither—
I suspect—go venturing thither,
Wreak destruction, wreck, and raze
Rat-bitats aplenty. Well
In a certain year, when flourished
Ratdom's populace, well-nourished,
Lo! their sovereign, Rat le Bel, [1]
Raised an army and attacked
(Though in self-defense, in fact!);
And, beneath their unfurled banner,
Weasles countered in like manner.
Each side hacked, slashed, pillaged, sacked…
If we can believe reports,
Victory long remained in doubt
As the blood of both cohorts—
Shedding, spreading roundabout—
Rendered fertile many a bare and
Fallow field. But *c'est la guerre*, and
One side always dies the most.
Now, the Ratovingian host

Sa déroute fut entiere,
Quoy que pust faire Artarpax,
Psicarpax, Meridarpax,
Qui, tout couverts de poussiere,
Soûtinrent assez long-temps
Les efforts des combattans.
Leur resistance fut vaine:
Il falut ceder au sort.
Chacun s'enfuit au plus fort,
Tant Soldat que Capitaine.
Les Princes perirent tous.
La racaille dans des trous
Trouvant sa retraite preste,
Se sauva sans grand travail.
Mais les Seigneurs sur leur teste
Ayant chacun un plumail,
Des cornes ou des aigrettes,
Soit comme marques d'honneur,
Soit afin que les Belettes
En conçussent plus de peur:
Cela causa leur malheur.
Trou, ny fente, ny crevasse,
Ne fut large assez pour eux,
Au lieu que la populace
Entroit dans les moindres creux.
La principale jonchée
Fut donc des principaux Rats.
Une teste empanachée
N'est pas petit embarras.
Le trop superbe équipage
Peut souvent en un passage
Causer du retardement.
Les petits en toute affaire
Esquivent fort aisément;
Les grands ne le peuvent faire.

Was, alas, that side undone,
Routed by the adversary,
Crushed despite much military
Prowess shown by many a one—
Artarpax, Meridarpax,
Psicharpax by name,[2] who, gallant,
Game, long staved off their attacks.
But in vain, for all their talent
Tactical in ways of war,
All these captains, privates—touched
By defeat—begrimed, besmutched—
Suffered Fate's decrees. What's more,
Though the poor paw-sloggers fled,
Safe in their retreat, quite dead
All the royal household perished.
Why? Because each princely head
Bore some precious plume, some cherished
Gewgaw, knick-knack, decoration,
Either as an honorific
Emblem, or a mark horrific
Meant to spread great consternation
Weaselwards. But only woe
Did it cause: plain folk had no
Trouble—being lithe and thin—
Slipping into crevice, crack,
Hole, or hollow; but, alack!
None was wide enough wherein
Those emplumed could safely hide:
Whence this dire rodenticide.
Thus it should be altogether
Clear that too much fuss and feather
Harms, not helps. For so much pride
Holds the great tight to their tether;
While the small, unprepossessing,
Find their modest size a blessing.

IV, 6

Le Cheval S'Estant Voulu Vanger du Cerf

De tout temps les Chevaux ne sont nez pour les hommes.
Lors que le genre humain de glan se contentoit,
Asne, Cheval, et Mule aux forests habitoit;
Et l'on ne voyoit point, comme au siecle où nous sommes,
    Tant de selles et tant de basts,
    Tant de harnois pour les combats,
    Tant de chaises, tant de carosses;
    Comme aussi ne voyoit-on pas
    Tant de festins et tant de nôces.
  Or un Cheval eut alors different
    Avec un Cerf plein de vîtesse,
  Et ne pouvant l'attraper en courant,
Il eut recours à l'Homme, implora son adresse.
L'Homme luy mit un frein, luy sauta sur le dos,
    Ne luy donna point de repos
Que le Cerf ne fust pris, et n'y laissast la vie.
  Et cela fait, le Cheval remercie
L'Homme son bien-faiteur, disant: Je suis à vous,
Adieu. Je m'en retourne en mon sejour sauvage.
—Non pas cela, dit l'Homme, il fait meilleur chez nous:
    Je vois trop quel est vostre usage.
  Demeurez donc, vous serez bien traité,
    Et jusqu'au ventre en la litiere.

    Helas! que sert la bonne chere
    Quand on n'a pas la liberté?
Le cheval s'apperçut qu'il avoit fait folie;
Mais il n'estoit plus temps: déja son écurie
    Estoit prête et toute bâtie.
  Il y mourut en traînant son lien.
Sage s'il eût remis une legere offense.
Quel que soit le plaisir que cause la vengeance,
C'est l'acheter trop cher, que l'acheter d'un bien
    Sans qui les autres ne sont rien.

The Horse Who Sought Revenge on the Stag

The horse has not served Man since time began.
Back in our forest days, dark days of yore,
    When, perforce, ass, mule, horse—and Man—
    Lived but on acorns, little more,
    We had no need for such as saddle,
    Harness for war, bit, pack, or all
    Our costly carriage folderol
    Fit for today's fine fiddle-faddle.
Back then, it came to pass a certain horse,
Fresh from a squabble with a stag, though fleet
Of hoof, yet failed to catch him; thought it meet,
    In his duress, to have recourse
To Man; begged him to help him with his skill.
Man gave his jaws a bit; fashioned some reins;
Jumped on his back, and urged him on until
    The stag lay caught. After the kill,
    Thanking the man for all his pains:
"I'm much obliged," the stallion says, and goes
To leave, back to his wild domains. "Adieu."
"Nay nay," the man replies. "Let me propose,
Friend, that you ought remain with me. Here, you
Will have naught but the finest board and bed."

    What does it matter how well fed
    Or how well bedded one might be
If, for the boon, one pays his liberty?
    The horse soon learned he'd lost his head:
    Too late! Already built, the stable
Was to become his final home: unable
Ever to break his bonds, there would he end
    His days. How much more prudent if
He had but overlooked his silly tiff.
For all the pleasure vengeance brings, to spend
    A fee so high is folly. Fie! It
Isn't worth what we hold most dear to buy it.

IV, 13

Le Renard et le Buste

Les Grands, pour la pluspart, sont masques de theatre;
Leur apparence impose au vulgaire idolâtre.
L'Asne n'en sçait juger que parce qu'il en void.
Le Renard au contraire à fonds les examine,
Les tourne de tout sens; et quand il s'apperçoit
    Que leur fait n'est que bonne mine,
Il leur applique un mot qu'un Buste de Heros
    Luy fit dire fort à propos.
C'estoit un Buste creux, et plus grand que nature.
Le Renard en loüant l'effort de la Sculpture,
Belle teste, dit-il, *mais de cervelle point.*
Combien de grands Seigneurs sont Bustes en ce point?

The Fox and the Bust

Nobles are often merely theatre masks.
The vulgar masses, awed, bow low. The ass's
Judgment is formed by what he sees: he asks
   No more; whereas the fox, probes, passes
Before, behind, beside… all round. And when
   He finds them to be naught but show,
   Then does he utter once again
   A most appropriate *bon mot*;
   One he once said, if I recall,
About a hero's bust wrought by some master,
Larger than life, but hollow—quite—withal:
"A handsome head; but brains? No, none at all."
How many a noble is mere empty plaster!

IV, 14

L'Oracle et l'Impie

Vouloir tromper le Ciel, c'est folie à la Terre;
Le Dedale des cœurs en ses détours n'enserre
Rien qui ne soit d'abord éclairé par les Dieux.
Tout ce que l'homme fait, il le fait à leurs yeux,
Même les actions que dans l'ombre il croit faire.
Un Payen qui sentoit quelque peu le fagot,
Et qui croyoit en Dieu, pour user de ce mot,
     Par benefice d'inventaire,
     Alla consulter Apollon.
     Dés qu'il fut en son sanctuaire:
Ce que je tiens, dit-il, est-il en vie ou non?
     Il tenoit un moineau, dit-on,
     Prest d'étouffer la pauvre beste,
     Ou de la lâcher aussi-tost,
     Pour mettre Apollon en défaut.
Apollon reconnut ce qu'il avoit en teste.
Mort ou vif, luy dit-il, montre-nous ton moineau,
     Et ne me tends plus de panneau;
Tu te trouverois mal d'un pareil stratagême.
     Je vois de loin, j'atteins de même.

The Oracle and the Infidel

To seek to fool the gods is folly arrant:
The labyrinthine crannies of Man's heart,
Disguise them though he try, with cleverest art,
    Appear before them, clear, transparent.
In fact, his every deed, his every act,
However darkly done, rises intact
    Before their eyes. And so my story:
A rustic infidel, a heathen (yet
One who took stock of heaven, to hedge his bet!)
    Went to Apollo's oratory—
The oracle, that is—and, once inside
    The holy precincts, boldly cried:
"Tell me, is what I'm holding in my fist
Dead or alive?" Our demi-atheist
Held, so they say, a sparrow; one that he,
    At the god's answer, could set free
    Or smother utterly, thereby
Proving him wrong, whichever his reply.
Seeing his plan, "Come now," Apollo said.
"Fie on your foolish traps! Alive or dead,
Show us your sparrow!… See? My sight is strong.
And, what is more, beware: My arm is long!"

IV, 19

L'Œil du Maistre

Un Cerf s'estant sauvé dans une estable à bœufs
    Fut d'abord averty par eux
    Qu'il cherchât un meilleur azile.
Mes freres, leur dit-il, ne me decelez pas:
Je vous enseigneray les pâtis les plus gras;
Ce service vous peut quelque jour estre utile;
    Et vous n'en aurez point regret.
Les Bœufs à toutes fins promirent le secret.
Il se cache en un coin, respire, et prend courage.
Sur le soir on apporte herbe fraische et fourage

The Master's Eye

A stag sought refuge with the race bovine
    Inside a barn. The oxen thought,
    All things considered, that he ought
    Best seek another. "Brothers mine,"
    I pray you, do a kindly deed
    And not betray me! By and by
I'll show you where to find the tastiest feed!"
    His oxen hosts agree, comply
    With his request for sanctuary.
Off in a corner, much relieved, and very
Grateful, he hides… The servants come, that night,

67

Comme l'on faisoit tous les jours.
L'on va, l'on vient, les valets font cent tours,
L'Intendant mesme, et pas un d'avanture
N'apperçût ny corps ny ramure,
Ny Cerf enfin. L'habitant des forests
Rend déja grace aux Bœufs, attend dans cette étable
Que chacun retournant au travail de Cerés,
Il trouve pour sortir un moment favorable.
L'un des Bœufs ruminant luy dit: Cela va bien;
Mais quoy! l'homme aux cent yeux n'a pas fait sa reveuë.
Je crains fort pour toy sa venuë.
Jusques-là, pauvre Cerf, ne te vante de rien.
Là-dessus le Maistre entre et vient faire sa ronde.
Qu'est-ce cy? dit-il à son monde.
Je trouve bien peu d'herbe en tous ces rateliers!
Cette litiere est vieille; allez vîte aux greniers.
Je veux voir desormais vos bestes mieux soignées.
Que couste-t-il d'oster toutes ces araignées?
Ne sçauroit-on ranger ces jougs et ces colliers?
En regardant à tout, il voit une autre tête
Que celles qu'il voyoit d'ordinaire en ce lieu.
Le Cerf est reconnu; chacun prend un épieu;
Chacun donne un coup à la beste.
Ses larmes ne sçauroient la sauver du trépas.
On l'emporte, on la sale, on en fait maint repas,
Dont maint voisin s'éjoüit d'estre.
Phedre, sur ce sujet, dit fort élegamment:
Il n'est pour voir que l'œil du Maître.
Quant à moy, j'y mettrois encor l'œil de l'Amant.

With fodder… Come, go… In, out… But despite
  The hubbub and the feeding fuss,
Stewart and minions are oblivious
To antlered head (and stag *in toto!*). Quite
Thankful, the forest denizen waits, bides
His time until the varlets leave, to labor,
  Tilling fair Ceres'[1] field; decides
  Now is the time to go. "But, neighbor,"
Bellows an ox, chewing his cud. "Poor deer!
  Till now you've had no dealings, none,
With him we call 'the hundred-eyeballed one!'
  Don't be so brash, so cavalier!
Until he comes, himself, to check the herd,
The barn, and all, you haven't heard the end,
I fear!" No sooner had that final word
  Parted his lips than—heaven forfend!—
  In stalks the master; makes his rounds…
  "What's this?" he cries. "Gadzooks and zounds!
Look at this filthy litter!… Change it please!…
  Go get more fodder!… What are these
  Yokes doing here?… And tell me, why
Must there be spiders everywhere?…" And on
And on he rants and cavils; whereupon,
  Darting his glance, his eyes espy
An unknown head. Alas, our stag lies caught.
Mid pikes and spears, tears, pleas go all for naught!
They kill him, salt him… Many a mouth will feast
  For many a day upon our beast.
Phædrus it was who proved the point concisely:
"The master's eye is best!"[2] he put it nicely.
(Myself, I'll add another's, *con amore*:
The lover's too! But that's another story!)

IV, 21

L'Aloüette et Ses Petits,
avec le Maistre d'un Champ

Ne t'attens qu'à toy seul, c'est un commun Proverbe.
      Voicy comme Esope le mit
           En credit.
      Les Aloüettes font leur nid
      Dans les bleds quand ils sont en herbe,
      C'est-à-dire environ le temps
Que tout aime, et que tout pullule dans le monde:
      Monstres marins au fond de l'onde,
Tigres dans les Forests, Aloüettes aux champs.
      Une pourtant de ces dernieres
Avoit laissé passer la moitié d'un Printemps
Sans gouster le plaisir des amours printanieres.
A toute force enfin elle se resolut
D'imiter la Nature, et d'estre mere encore.
Elle bâtit un nid, pond, couve et fait éclore
A la haste; le tout alla du mieux qu'il put.
Les bleds d'alentour mûrs, avant que la nitée
      Se trouvast assez forte encor
      Pour voler et prendre l'essor,
De mille soins divers l'Aloüette agitée
S'en va chercher pâture, avertit ses enfans
D'estre toujours au guet et faire sentinelle.
      Si le possesseur de ces champs
Vient avecque son fils (comme il viendra), dit-elle,
    Ecoutez bien; selon ce qu'il dira,
      Chacun de nous décampera.
Si-tost que l'Aloüette eut quitté sa famille,
Le possesseur du champ vient avecque son fils.
Ces bleds sont mûrs, dit-il, allez chez nos amis
Les prier que chacun, apportant sa faucille,

The Lark, Her Little Ones, and the Farmer Who Owns the Field

"Count not on others!" Thus our antecedents
    Wisely advised us to behave.
Common the adage. Here's how Æsop gave
        It credence. [1]
    Each year the larks would build their nest
Amid the stalks of grain budding to life;
    That season green when, passion-rife,
A teeming Nature—birds, plants, all the rest
Of livingkind—gives way to love: sweet spring.
    Beasts all, and all with but one notion:
    Monsters beneath the briny ocean,
Tigers of forest climes, larks on the wing…
    One of the latter, for some reason
    Deaf to the urgings of the season
    Until it was, alas, half past,
    Decided it was time, at last,
To taste the joys of springtime love, and do
Like earth and Nature, and give birth anew.
Quickly she builds her nest, lays, sits… Anon,
She hatches out her brood; but, spring now gone,
The wheat whereon they nested had already
Ripened before the hatchlings—too unsteady,
    Too weak of wing yet to take flight—
    Had learned to go in search of food.
    Wherefore, with much solicitude,
The mother lark, eager to ease their plight,
    Goes foraging; but not before
Proffering words of warning by the score,
Telling them they must keep a well-peeled eye
In case Monsieur, who owns the field, comes by:

Nous vienne aider demain dés la pointe du jour.
     Nostre Aloüette de retour
     Trouve en alarme sa couvée.
L'un commence: Il a dit que l'Aurore levée,
L'on fist venir demain ses amis pour l'aider…
—S'il n'a dit que cela, repartit l'Aloüette,
Rien ne nous presse encor de changer de retraite;
Mais c'est demain qu'il faut tout de bon écouter.
Cependant soyez gais; voilà dequoy manger.
Eux repus, tout s'endort, les petits et la mere.
L'aube du jour arrive; et d'amis point du tout.
L'Aloüette à l'essort, le Maistre s'en vient faire
     Sa ronde ainsi qu'à l'ordinaire.
Ces bleds ne devroient pas, dit-il, estre debout.
Nos amis ont grant tort, et tort qui se repose
Sur de tels paresseux à servir ainsi lents.
     Mon fils, allez chez nos parens
     Les prier de la mesme chose.
L'épouvante est au nid plus forte que jamais.
Il a dit ses parens, mere, c'est à cette heure…
     —Non, mes enfans, dormez en paix;
     Ne bougeons de nôtre demeure.
L'Aloüette eut raison, car personne ne vint.
Pour la troisiéme fois le Maistre se souvint
De visiter ses bleds. Nostre erreur est extrême,
Dit-il, de nous attendre à d'autres gens que nous.
Il n'est meilleur ami ni parent que soy-mesme.
Retenez bien cela, mon fils; et sçavez-vous
Ce qu'il faut faire? Il faut qu'avec nostre famille
Nous prenions dés demain chacun une faucille:
C'est là nostre plus court, et nous acheverons

"He and his son," she says, "as they
Most surely will." Then, adding: "Listen well!
    For, truly, what he has to say
Can seal our fate." She leaves, and, truth to tell,
Monsieur appears next moment with said son.
"The wheat is ripe. Go ask our friends, each one,"
Says he, "to bring a sickle and come here
At dawn to help us." Soon our lark returns,
    Finds her brood much alarmed, and learns
    Quickly the reason for their fear.
" 'At dawn,' he said… With all his friends… Tomorrow…"
"Indeed? If that was all he said, no worry!
    Come feed on what I've found. No hurry!
Surely we have no need to go and borrow
Trouble just yet. Tomorrow, once again,
We'll listen well and, maybe, worry then."
    Meanwhile they supped, then slept… Next day,
    Dawn breaks. And friends? No, none… Off flies
    The mother. Comes Monsieur: "I say,"
Says he, "my wheat still standing? Ah," he sighs,
"What worthless friends! What good-for-nothing wretches!
Go fetch my cousins all!" And, in the nest,
    Our fledgelings, still more sore distressed:
    "Now cousins… Cousins, now he fetches…
Cousins galore he's sending for!…" Another
"Tut tut" of reassurance from the mother:
    "Sleep tight. We have no cause to flee."
And right she was. Cousins? Not one… The third
    Day, when Monsieur came eagerly
To view his crop, these were the words they heard:
"What fools we are to count on others! We

Nostre moisson quand nous pourrons.
Dés-lors que ce dessein fut sceu de l'Aloüette:
C'est ce coup qu'il est bon de partir, mes enfans.
Et les petits en mesme temps,
Voletans, se culebutans,
Délogerent tous sans trompette.

Can count on but ourselves, you hear?
Tomorrow we—no neighbors, brothers, kin—
Will come, each with our sickle, and begin
Our labors, best we can." The lark gave ear.
"Now is the time," she tells her brood. And they
Flutter, untrumpeted, and fly away.

IV, 22

75

Les Oreilles du Lievre

Un animal cornu blessa de quelques coups
  Le Lion, qui plein de couroux,
  Pour ne plus tomber en la peine,
  Bannit des lieux de son domaine
Toute beste portant des cornes à son front.
Chevres, Beliers, Taureaux aussi-tost délogerent,
  Daims, et Cerfs de climat changerent;
  Chacun à s'en aller fut prompt.
Un Lievre, appercevant l'ombre de ses oreilles,
  Craignit que quelque Inquisiteur
N'allast interpreter à cornes leur longueur,
Ne les soûtinst en tout à des cornes pareilles.
Adieu, voisin Grillon, dit-il, je pars d'icy;
Mes oreilles enfin seroient cornes aussi;
Et quand je les aurois plus courtes qu'une Autruche,
Je craindrois mesme encor. Le Grillon repartit:
  Cornes cela? Vous me prenez pour cruche;
  Ce sont oreilles que Dieu fit.
   —On les fera passer pour cornes,
Dit l'animal craintif, et cornes de Licornes.
J'auray beau protester; mon dire et mes raisons
  Iront aux petites Maisons.

The Hare and His Ears

The lion was, in ages past, attacked
By some horned animal. The aftermath
   Was such that, in his kingly wrath,
   He thought it well that he enact
An edict whereby every beast who sported
Horns of whatever kind must be deported.
   In fact, goat, ram, deer, hind, and bull—
Most disinclined to stay, though sorrowful
   That they must fly—each fled his lair.
   Fearful and most distressed, a hare,
Seeing the shadow of his ears, feared they
Be taken by some court inquisitor
For horns; and thus decided that, before
They were, indeed, best he be on his way.
"Friend cricket, I must leave," says he. "Bye bye.
I worry lest they misperceive, and see
   My ears as two long horns! Why, I
Could have small ostrich-ears; still should I be
Afraid!" The cricket answers: "Me oh my!
   You take me for a fool? Those? Horns?
   God made you ears, and ears is what
They are!" The timid hare retorted: "But
They'll call them horns! Even two unicorns'!
   Say what I please, I know their tricks:
They'll lock me up with all the lunatics!"[1]

V, 4

77

La Vieille et les Deux Servantes

Il estoit une vieille ayant deux Chambrieres.
Elles filoient si bien que les sœurs filandieres
Ne faisoient que broüiller au prix de celles-cy.
La Vieille n'avoit point de plus pressant soucy
Que de distribuer aux Servantes leur tâche.
Dés que Thetis chassoit Phœbus aux crins dorez,
Tourets entroient en jeu, fuseaux estoient tirez,
  Deçà, delà, vous en aurez;
  Point de cesse, point de relâche.
Dés que l'Aurore, dis-je, en son char remontoit,
Un miserable Coq à poinct nommé chantoit.
Aussi-tost nostre Vieille encor plus miserable
S'affubloit d'un jupon crasseux et detestable,
Allumoit une lampe, et couroit droit au lit
Où de tout leur pouvoir, de tout leur appetit,
  Dormoient les deux pauvres Servantes.
L'une entr'ouvroit un œil, l'autre étendoit un bras;
  Et toutes deux, tres-mal contentes,
Disoient entre leurs dents: Maudit Coq, tu mourras.
Comme elles l'avoient dit, la beste fut gripée.
Le Réveille-matin eut la gorge coupée.
Ce meurtre n'amanda nullement leur marché.
Nostre couple au contraire à peine estoit couché
Que la Vieille, craignant de laisser passer l'heure,
Couroit comme un Lutin par toute sa demeure.
  C'est ainsi que le plus souvent,
Quand on pense sortir d'une mauvaise affaire,
  On s'enfonce encor plus avant:
  Témoin ce Couple et son salaire.
La Vieille au lieu du Coq les fit tomber par là
  De Caribde en Sylla.

The Old Woman and the Two Servants

Once, an old woman had two maids, the kind
That spin; and spin they did: cloth so well done
That the three spinning sister-Fates combined
Were vulgar drudges in comparison. [1]
Each day she had no care more pressing, none,
   Than to distribute to the pair
Their tasks: as Phœbus, rising through the air—
He of the golden locks—quit Tethys' sea, [2]
Lo! In a frenzy of activity
   Spindles dart to and fro, wheels turn,
Unceasing… Why? Because, as I have mentioned,
When dawn commenced its chariot-drawn sojourn,
A certain cock, wretched and vile-intentioned,
   Would crow his call. The hag, as vile,
Would don a grease-bespattered shift, meanwhile
Lighting her lamp, and run, fast as she could,
Straight to the bed where our two spinsters would
Gladly have slept the day away. [3] The first
Squinted an eye, the other stretched an arm.
   Both vowed between clenched teeth that harm
Would come to that damned cock, that fowl accurse

   Thus, with the scorn that so befit it,
Seizing the morning-crier's throat, they slit it.
Said murder, though, failed to improve their lot:
   No sooner had the couple got
To sleep again than, quick, our harridan,
Elf-like, afraid to miss the dawn, began
To run about, here, there, and everywhere!
Thus, often, do we pay for our desire
To raise ourselves out of some fell affair,
Only to sink still deeper in the mire!
The proof? Our pair, and she who thus harassed them:
   For hag it was, not cock, who cast them
Out of the frying-pan, into the fire!

V, 6

79

Le Satyre et le Passant

Au fond d'un antre sauvage,
Un Satyre et ses enfans
Alloient manger leur potage
Et prendre l'écuelle aux dents.

On les eust vûs sur la mousse
Luy, sa femme, et maint petit;
Ils n'avoient tapis ni housse,
Mais tous fort bon appetit.

Pour se sauver de la pluye
Entre un Passant morfondu.
Au broüet on le convie;
Il n'estoit pas attendu.

Son hoste n'eut pas la peine
De le semondre deux fois;
D'abord avec son haleine
Il se réchauffe les doits.

Puis sur le mets qu'on luy donne
Delicat il souffle aussi;
Le Satyre s'en étonne:
Nostre hoste, à quoy bon cecy?

The Satyr and the Passerby

In a desert cave, a satyr [1]
And his godforsaken troop—
Many an offspring, mater, pater—
Were about to sup their soup,

Sprawling on the mosses there.
Ah! Could you have seen the sight!
Ground uncovered, bodies bare…
Oh, but what an appetite!

Whereupon a passerby,
Freezing from the rain, soaked through,
Wanders in, no doubt to dry,
Uninvited; still, our crew

Offer him some gruel. The guest
Needs no second invitation;
Blows upon his hands, hard-pressed
To restore their circulation;

Then blows on his soup—but very
Gently; and that host of his,
At this conduct most contrary,
Asks him what the reason is.

—L'un refroidit mon potage,
L'autre réchauffe ma main.
—Vous pouvez, dit le Sauvage,
Reprendre vostre chemin.

Ne plaise aux Dieux que je couche
Avec vous sous mesme toit.
Arriere ceux dont la bouche
Souffle le chaud et le froid!

"First I blow to warm my hands,
Then to cool my food." "I see!"
And the woodland beast commands:
"Then please leave, immediately!

"Ye gods! I'll not share my shelter
With some creature misbegot;
One whose mouth will, helter-skelter,
Now blow cold and now blow hot."

Le Cheval et le Loup

Un certain Loup, dans la saison
Que les tiedes Zephyrs ont l'herbe rajeunie,
Et que les animaux quittent tous la maison,
        Pour s'en aller chercher leur vie;
Un Loup, dis-je, au sortir des rigueurs de l'Hyver,
Apperceut un Cheval qu'on avoit mis au vert.
        Je laisse à penser quelle joye!
Bonne chasse, dit-il, qui l'auroit à son croc.
Eh! que n'es-tu Mouton? car tu me serois hoc:
Au lieu qu'il faut ruser pour avoir cette proye.
Rusons donc. Ainsi dit, il vient à pas comptez,
        Se dit Ecolier d'Hippocrate;
Qu'il connoist les vertus et les proprietez
        De tous les Simples de ces prez;
        Qu'il sçait guerir, sans qu'il se flate,
Toutes sortes de maux. Si Dom Coursier vouloit
        Ne point celer sa maladie,
        Luy Loup gratis le gueriroit.
        Car le voir en cette prairie
        Paistre ainsi sans estre lié
Témoignoit quelque mal, selon la Medecine.
        J'ay, dit la Beste chevaline,
        Une apostume sous le pied.
—Mon fils, dit le Docteur, il n'est point de partie
        Susceptible de tant de maux.
J'ay l'honneur de servir Nosseigneurs les Chevaux,
        Et fais aussi la Chirurgie.
Mon galand ne songeoit qu'à bien prendre son temps,
        Afin de haper son malade.
L'autre qui s'en doutoit luy lâche une ruade,
        Qui vous luy met en marmelade

The Horse and the Wolf

That season, when the Southwind blows the grass
    To green once more; when zephyrs' breath
Awakens Nature from her frigid death;
When creatures venture forth from hole, crevasse,
And den, quitting their wintry regimen
    To seek again their fortune; then
A wolf there was—to make my story short—
Who, putting winter's chill, perforce, behind,
Spying a horse set out to graze, opined
(Imagine with what glee!): "Ah, what fine sport!"
And, yearning for its flesh between his jaws:
    "Ah me," he mused, "why can't you be
    A sheep? I'd have you, one, two, three!
Instead, I'll have to use my wit, because
No easy prey is this. Beasts such as these
Seldom submit. Well, wit it is!" And thus,
With measured gait and tone obsequious:
"Good day! A student of Hippocrates
    To serve you, sire," he said, "and cure
    Your every ill with plant and herb,
Gratis, with Hippocratic skill superb.
For I suspect, my noble steed, that you're
Suffering something; else why, free, unreined,
Do you graze here?" (So did his science teach him!)
    No more, indeed, need wolf beseech him:
"True," said the horse, "I'll tell you." And he deigned
Reveal he had a tumor on his hoof.
Our sham physician sighed a soul-felt "Ouf!"
Saying: "There's no more tender spot. I'll heal it,
Surgically; for surgeon have I been,
Serving the royal stables, monsieur's kin.
    Come, valliant stallion, let me feel it."
Licking his chops, he coveted his meal: it
Wouldn't be long… But, much to his chagrin,

Les mendibules et les dents.
C'est bien fait, dit le Loup en soy-mesme fort triste;
Chacun à son métier doit toûjours s'attacher.
Tu veux faire icy l'Arboriste,
Et ne fus jamais que Boucher.

Our horse, with well-placed hoof, lashed out so well, he
Promptly reduced the lupine jaws to jelly.
"It serves me right," the wolf, supine and humbled,
    In a dejected murmur, mumbled.
"Professionally speaking, best persist
In what we know. For all your life you plied
    The butcher's trade. Why, now, decide
    To try and play the herbalist?"

V, 8

Le Laboureur et Ses Enfans

Travaillez, prenez de la peine:
C'est le fonds qui manque le moins.
Un riche Laboureur, sentant sa mort prochaine,
Fit venir ses enfans, leur parla sans témoins.
Gardez-vous, leur dit-il, de vendre l'heritage,
Que nous ont laissé nos parens.
Un tresor est caché dedans.
Je ne sçai pas l'endroit; mais un peu de courage
Vous le fera trouver, vous en viendrez à bout.
Remuez vostre champ dés qu'on aura fait l'Oust.
Creusez, foüillez, bêchez, ne laissez nulle place
Où la main ne passe et repasse.
Le pere mort, les fils vous retournent le champ
Deçà, delà, par tout; si bien qu'au bout de l'an
Il en rapporta davantage.
D'argent, point de caché. Mais le pere fut sage
De leur montrer avant sa mort
Que le travail est un tresor.

The Ploughman and His Sons

Work hard, hard as you can: then shall you
Learn that in work one finds the surest value.
    A wealthy ploughman, sensing death
Approach, sent for his children so that he
    Might counsel them in privacy,
    Telling them, with his dying breath:
"Beware never to sell this land that we
Inherited from forebears past. For, in it,
Buried, a hidden treasure lies. I know
Not where; but if you dig, and delve, and hoe,
Turning the earth and ploughing deep within it,
Certain you are to find it, come the autumn."
The father died... The sons ploughed top to bottom,
    Here, there—never an idle minute—
    Hoed, tilled... So well that, for their toil,
They sowed and reaped a bounty from the soil.
And buried treasure? Not a bit. That is,
No gold. But from the old man's deathbed wit—
    That fatherly advice of his—
They learned that work's the treasure. Cherish it.

V, 9

La Fortune et le Jeune Enfant

Sur le bord d'un puits tres-profond
Dormoit étendu de son long
Un Enfant alors dans ses classes.
Tout est aux Ecoliers couchette et matelas.
Un honneste homme en pareil cas
Auroit fait un saut de vingt brasses.
Prés de là tout heureusement
La Fortune passa, l'éveilla doucement,
Luy disant: Mon mignon, je vous sauve la vie.
Soyez une autre fois plus sage, je vous prie.
Si vous fussiez tombé, l'on s'en fust pris à moy;
Cependant c'estoit vostre faute.
Je vous demande en bonne foy
Si cette imprudence si haute
Provient de mon caprice. Elle part à ces mots.
Pour moy, j'approuve son propos.
Il n'arrive rien dans le monde
Qu'il ne faille qu'elle en réponde.
Nous la faisons de tous Echos.
Elle est prise à garand de toutes avantures.
Est-on sot, étourdi, prend-on mal ses mesures;
On pense en estre quitte en accusant son sort.
Bref la Fortune a toûjours tort.

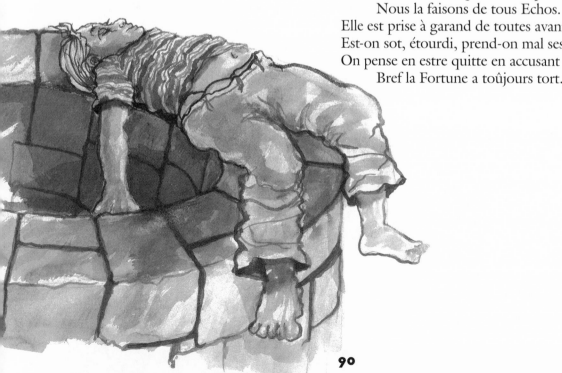

Dame Fortune and the Child

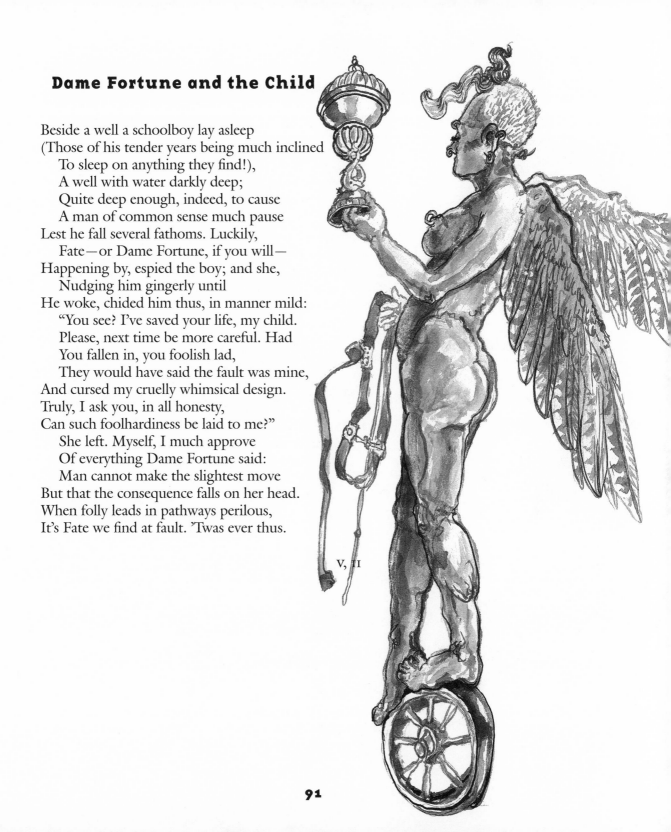

Beside a well a schoolboy lay asleep
(Those of his tender years being much inclined
   To sleep on anything they find!),
   A well with water darkly deep;
   Quite deep enough, indeed, to cause
   A man of common sense much pause
Lest he fall several fathoms. Luckily,
   Fate—or Dame Fortune, if you will—
Happening by, espied the boy; and she,
   Nudging him gingerly until
He woke, chided him thus, in manner mild:
   "You see? I've saved your life, my child.
   Please, next time be more careful. Had
   You fallen in, you foolish lad,
   They would have said the fault was mine,
And cursed my cruelly whimsical design.
Truly, I ask you, in all honesty,
Can such foolhardiness be laid to me?"
   She left. Myself, I much approve
   Of everything Dame Fortune said:
   Man cannot make the slightest move
But that the consequence falls on her head.
When folly leads in pathways perilous,
It's Fate we find at fault. 'Twas ever thus.

V, II

91

Le Liévre et la Perdrix

Il ne se faut jamais moquer des miserables:
Car qui peut s'asseurer d'estre toûjours heureux?
    Le sage Esope dans ses Fables
    Nous en donne un exemple ou deux.
    Celuy qu'en ces Vers je propose,
    Et les siens, ce sont mesme chose.
Le Liévre et la Perdrix, concitoyens d'un champ,
Vivoient dans un état, ce semble, assez tranquille,
    Quand une Meute s'approchant
Oblige le premier à chercher un azile.
Il s'enfuit dans son fort, met les chiens en défaut,
    Sans mesme en excepter Briffaut.
    Enfin il se trahit luy-mesme
Par les esprits sortans de son corps échauffé.
Miraut sur leur odeur ayant philosophé
Conclut que c'est son Liévre, et d'une ardeur extrême
Il le pousse, et Rustaut, qui n'a jamais menti,
    Dit que le Liévre est reparti.
Le pauvre malheureux vient mourir à son giste.
    La Perdrix le raille, et luy dit;
    Tu te vantois d'estre si vîte:
Qu'as-tu fait de tes pieds? Au moment qu'elle rit,
Son tour vient; on la trouve. Elle croit que ses aisles
La sçauront garentir à toute extremité;
    Mais la pauvrette avoit compté
    Sans l'Autour aux serres cruelles.

The Hare and the Partridge

Never should we make fun of those
Less fortunate than we. Who knows
How long our own felicity
Will last? Indeed, wise Æsop shows a few
Examples in his fables—one or two;
And I as well, no less than he,
Do likewise in these verses. Mine, like his,
Prove how perverse such conduct is.
The hare and partridge had been living, very
Peaceably, side by side, when lo! a pack
Of hounds appears! The hare, fearing attack,
Flees to his fortress, there to bury
Himself in safety. Hounds are left, high, dry!
Even Briffaut the Glutton!…[1] By and by,
Alas, the hare betrays himself, exuding
Scents that the heat sends rising from his lair.
Miraut the Sharp-Eyed, sniffing, and concluding
That therebelow must lurk the hare,
Pokes at his hole. As for Rustaut the Wise,
He disagrees: "There's no more hare down there!"
So long do they philosophize,
That, in his burrow, trapped, the poor beast dies.
"Well now, where were those paws, those speedy feet
That flew so fast?" the partridge, quick to mock,
Guffaws. Secure is she, so firm and fleet
Of wing!… Ah, but she quite forgot the hawk,
He of the deadly claws! No more she'll scoff,
As down he swoops, and sweeps her off!

V, 17

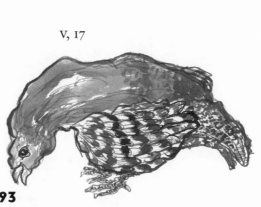

93

L'Aigle et le Hibou

L'Aigle et le Chat-huant leurs querelles cesserent,
    Et firent tant qu'ils s'embrasserent.
L'un jura foy de Roy, l'autre foy de Hibou,
Qu'ils ne se goberoient leurs petits peu ny prou.
Connoissez-vous les miens? dit l'Oiseau de Minerve.
—Non, dit l'Aigle.—Tant pis, reprit le triste Oiseau.
    Je crains en ce cas pour leur peau:
    C'est hazard si je les conserve.
Comme vous estes Roy, vous ne considerez
Qui ny quoy: Rois et Dieux mettent, quoy qu'on leur die,
    Tout en mesme categorie.

The Eagle and the Owl

Two enemies, the screech owl and the eagle,
Eager to live in peace, embraced and swore
   That neither one would, evermore,
Feed on the other's chicks. "I give my regal
Word," vowed the latter; and the former hooted:
"Owl's honor!" And Minerva's bird went on:
"Do you know mine?" "No…" "Then I fear, anon,
   Your solemn promise will be mooted:
Should they survive, for all your good intent,
It will, I think, be but an accident.
A king you are; and kings, like gods, make no
   Distinction in their subjects; so
Woe to my young if you should find them." "Well,

Adieu mes nourriçons si vous les rencontrez.
—Peignez-les-moy, dit l'Aigle, ou bien me les montrez.
            Je n'y toucheray de ma vie.
Le Hibou repartit: Mes petits sont mignons,
Beaux, bien faits, et jolis sur tous leurs compagnons.
Vous les reconnoistrez sans peine à cette marque.
N'allez pas l'oublier; retenez-la si bien
            Que chez moy la maudite Parque
            N'entre point par vostre moyen.
Il avint qu'au Hibou Dieu donna geniture,
De façon qu'un beau soir qu'il estoit en pasture,
            Nostre Aigle apperceut d'avanture,
            Dans les coins d'une roche dure,
            Ou dans les trous d'une mazure,
            (Je ne sçais pas lequel des deux),
            De petits monstres fort hideux,
Rechignez, un air triste, une voix de Megere.
Ces enfans ne sont pas, dit l'Aigle, à nostre amy:
Croquons-les. Le galand n'en fit pas à demy.
Ses repas ne sont point repas à la legere.
Le Hibou de retour ne trouve que les pieds
De ses chers nourriçons, helas! pour toute chose.
Il se plaint, et les Dieux sont par luy suppliez
De punir le brigand qui de son deüil est cause.
Quelqu'un luy dit alors: N'en accuse que toy,
            Ou plustost la commune loy,
            Qui veut qu'on trouve son semblable
            Beau, bien fait, et sur tous aimable.
Tu fis de tes enfans à l'Aigle ce portrait;
            En avoient-ils le moindre trait?

In that case," said the eagle, "tell
Me what they look like; even show
Them; they'll be safe. I guarantee." The owl
Replied: "My babes? They're beautiful, the very
Picture of pure perfection aviary,
Unlike their peers, mere vulgar fowl.
That's how to recognize them. Nor
Must you forget, lest evil Fate, a-prowl,
Visit my nest with you, darken my door."
It happened that God gave the owl a brood.
One night, when she was off in search of food, [1]
The eagle, soaring in his flight,
Passing a rocky crag (or maybe
Some hoveled cranny), chanced to catch a sight
Of many an ugly—hideous!—hatchling baby,
Tucked in a nest, pathetic, and with quite
The most shrew-like of chirps. [2] "Surely," he thought,
Such misbegotten wretches, so ill wrought,
Can't be my friend's! Let's eat!" He ate…
Now, when an eagle eats, he neither pities,
Pardons, nor spares. The owl, disconsolate,
Returned… Gawked… Squawked: "What? All my pretties,
Dead?" Yes, a pile of spindly legs and feet
Lay as their sole remains. [3] "Ye gods," she hoots,
"Punish this miscreant, this king of brutes,
This cause of my despair!" "But why entreat
The gods?" somebody asks. "Foreswear your wrath;
The fault is yours, fell aftermath
Of common folly: namely, to assume
Our offspring share our fair, delightful features.
See? You misled friend eagle, whom
Your brood struck as the frightfulest of creatures!"

V, 18

Le Pâtre et le Lion
&
Le Lion et le Chasseur

Les Fables ne sont pas ce qu'elles semblent estre.
Le plus simple animal nous y tient lieu de Maistre.
Une Morale nuë apporte de l'ennuy;
Le conte fait passer le precepte avec luy.
En ces sortes de feinte il faut instruire et plaire,
Et conter pour conter me semble peu d'affaire.
C'est par cette raison qu'égayant leur esprit,
Nombre de gens fameux en ce genre ont écrit.
Tous ont fuy l'ornement et le trop d'étenduë
On ne voit point chez eux de parole perduë.
Phedre estoit si succint qu'aucuns l'en ont blâmé.
Esope en moins de mots s'est encore exprimé.
Mais sur tous certain Grec rencherit et se pique
      D'une élegance Laconique.
Il renferme toujours son conte en quatre Vers;
Bien ou mal, je le laisse à juger aux Experts.
Voyons-le avec Esope en un sujet semblable.
L'un ameine un Chasseur, l'autre un Pâtre en sa Fable.
J'ay suivi leur projet quant à l'évenement,
Y cousant en chemin quelque trait seulement.
Voicy comme à peu prés Esope le raconte.

Un Pâtre à ses Brebis trouvant quelque méconte,
Voulut à toute force attraper le Larron.
Il s'en va prés d'un antre, et tend à l'environ
Des laqs à prendre Loups, soupçonnant cette engeance.
      Avant que partir de ces lieux:
Si tu fais, disoit-il, ô Monarque des Dieux,
Que le drosle à ces laqs se prenne en ma presence
      Et que je goûte ce plaisir,

The Shepherd and the Lion
&
The Lion and the Hunter

Fables are not what they appear to be.
The merest animals can, pleasingly,
Instruct by deed, not dull advice: we swallow
Gladly their tales, whence must the precepts follow.
To teach, to please… Such is the aim twofold
Behind these fictions. For, if truth be told,
To do no more than entertain, to tell
A story for the story's sake seems, well,
A trifle frivolous. And of those many
Fabulists known to fame, there are not any
Who waste their breath on empty ornament
That has no useful, serious intent. [1]
Phædrus was so concise that some are prone
To criticize his fashion. And our own
Æsop, the earliest, had been still more
Pithily brief with his enfabled lore.
But one there was—a certain Greek [2]—whose verse,
 Even more elegant and terse,
Made him stand out with pride above the rest.
For, all his fables did he tell, compressed
In but four lines! Good? Bad? May the well-versed
Be judge. Let's take a tale that Æsop, first,
Related, then the latter. (One, a shepherd
Paints; one, a hunter.) As for me, I've peppered
Slightly my telling. But no matter. Thus:

In Æsop's tale a shepherd, much a-fuss,
A-fume at losing many a lamb and ewe,
Decides to catch the thief. What does he do?
Assuming someone of the wolfly race's
Foul inclination, off he goes, and places
Traps roundabout those creatures' lair. But then,
 Before he turns to leave the den:

Parmi vingt Veaux je veux choisir
Le plus gras, et t'en faire offrande.
A ces mots sort de l'antre un Lion grand et fort.
Le Pâtre se tapit, et dit à demy mort:
Que l'homme ne sçait guere, helas! ce qu'il demande!
Pour trouver le Larron qui détruit mon troupeau,
Et le voir en ces laqs pris avant que je parte,
O Monarque des Dieux, je t'ay promis un Veau:
Je te promets un Bœuf si tu fais qu'il s'écarte.
C'est ainsi que l'a dit le principal Auteur;
Passons à son imitateur.

Un Fanfaron amateur de la chasse,
Venant de perdre un Chien de bonne race,
Qu'il soupçonnoit dans le corps d'un Lion,
Vid un berger. Enseigne-moy, de grace,
De mon voleur, luy dit-il, la maison;
Que de ce pas je me fasse raison.
Le Berger dit: C'est vers cette montagne.
En luy payant de tribut un Mouton
Par chaque mois, j'erre dans la campagne
Comme il me plaist, et je suis en repos.
Dans le moment qu'ils tenoient ces propos,
Le Lion sort, et vient d'un pas agile.
Le Fanfaron aussi-tost d'esquiver.
O Jupiter, montre-moy quelque azile,
S'écria-t-il, qui me puisse sauver.

La vraye épreuve de courage
N'est que dans le danger que l'on touche du doigt.
Tel le cherchoit, dit-il, qui changeant de langage
S'enfuït aussi-tost qu'il le void.

"O sovereign of the gods," says he, "I pray
   You let me see my popinjay
   Caught here and now before my eyes.
   And if I have the final laugh,
   I promise you the fattest calf
In solemn sacrifice!" As thus he cries,
Out stalks a lion from the den! Half dead
With fright, the shepherd, once again: "Forget
The calf, good god! An ox! An ox, I said,
   Is yours if only you can get
This animal to leave and let me be!"
There's Æsop's tale. Now for his imitator:

A hunter—something of a perorator,
Boastful, brash—lost his dog: fine pedigree,
Good stock... Suspecting that the hound had been
Consumed, and that he now was lying in
A lion's belly, asked the hunter: "Where,
Pray tell, does that fell thief reside? It's my
Intent to punish him forthwith!" "Out there,
Off by the mountain," said a shepherd. "I
Pay him one sheep a month. That's how and why
I'm able to go anywhere I please."
As thus they speak, exchanging repartees,
Voilà! The lion saunters by. Our braggard,
Cringing now, turning pale and deathly haggard:
"Jupiter!" cries, "I beg you show me some
Close place to hide; if not my life is lost!"

   Courage is courage when the cost
Is high. "Some call for danger: let it come,"
Our poet says, "and off they fly, struck dumb."

VI, I, 2

101

Phœbus et Borée

Borée et le Soleil virent un Voyageur
    Qui s'étoit muny par bon-heur
Contre le mauvais temps. (On entroit dans l'Automne,
Quand la précaution aux Voyageurs est bonne)
Il pleut; le Soleil luit; et l'écharpe d'Iris
    Rend ceux qui sortent avertis
Qu'en ces mois le manteau leur est fort necessaire.
Les Latins les nommoient douteux pour cette affaire.
Nostre homme s'estoit donc à la pluye attendu:
Bon manteau bien doublé; bonne étoffe bien forte.
Celuy-cy, dit le Vent, prétend avoir pourvû
A tous les accidens; mais il n'a pas préveu
    Que je sçauray souffler de sorte
Qu'il n'est bouton qui tienne: il faudra, si je veux,
    Que le manteau s'en aille au Diable.
L'ébatement pourroit nous en estre agreable:
Vous plaist-il de l'avoir?—Et bien, gageons nous deux,
    (Dit Phœbus) sans tant de paroles,
A qui plustost aura dégarny les épaules
    Du Cavalier que nous voyons.
Commencez. Je vous laisse obscurcir mes rayons.
Il n'en fallut pas plus. Nostre souffleur à gage
Se gorge de vapeurs, s'enfle comme un balon,

Phœbus and Boreas [1]

One early autumn day, Northwind and Sun
Noticed a traveler, who was, happily,
Well-clothed against the weather. Everyone
Knows that in autumn—surely you agree—
   Prudence is a necessity:
   It rains; the sun comes out; and those
Who venture forth see Iris's hued bows
Spanning the sky, sign that they best had don
A coat or cloak. (Which is why, once upon
A time, the Latins said one should be wary,
   Come autumn, of this most capricious
Time of the year.) Now then, our solitary
   Traveler, decked in his judicious
   Garb, was well-clad in coat well-lined
   Of fabric tough, well-woven. "Ho
And hum!" gruff Northwind puffed. "He thinks he'll find
   Protection from what I've designed
   To send his way! Doesn't he know
There is no clasp, no button strong enough
To hold against the breaths I blow! One huff,
   And devil take his cloak! Indeed,
It might be quite the joke to see! What say?"
   "Fine!" answered Sun. "We really need

103

Fait un vacarme de demon,
Siffle, souffle, tempeste, et brise en son passage
Maint toit qui n'en peut mais, fait perir maint bateau:
Le tout au sujet du manteau.
Le Cavalier eut soin d'empêcher que l'orage
Ne se pût engoufrer dedans.
Cela le preserva; le vent perdit son temps:
Plus il se tourmentoit, plus l'autre tenoit ferme;
Il eut beau faire agir le colet et les plis.
Si-tost qu'il fut au bout du terme
Qu'à la gageure on avoit mis,
Le Soleil dissipe la nuë,
Recrée, et puis penetre enfin le Cavalier,
Sous son balandras fait qu'il suë,
Le contraint de s'en dépoüiller.
Encor n'usa-t-il pas de toute sa puissance.
Plus fait douceur que violence.

Not blather on, though. Rather, *s'il vous plaît,*
Let's bet which of us will be first to get
    Our friend to doff his coat." "Agreed!"
    Phœbus goes on: "I'll even let
Your storm clouds veil my rays. So, you begin."
And so begin he does. Cheeks puffed with rain,
He growls, blasts, bellows, and with hellish din
Blows roofs from housetops, howls his hurricane
Over the seas, until many a boat
Sinks to the bottom too! All for a coat!…
    The traveler parries every thrust,
Wrapped tighter with each gust, obstinately,
Till Northwind must admit, at length, that he
Has failed in the allotted time. And just
As he abates, Sun dissipates the shroud
Before his face; and, from behind the cloud,
Burns down upon our cavalier—though not
    Even with all his strength!—who, hot
And sweating, doffs his garment in due course.
One can do more with kindness than with force.

VI, 3

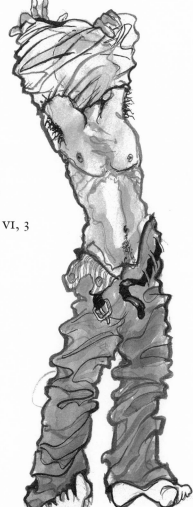

Le Cochet, le Chat,
et le Souriceau

Un Souriceau tout jeune, et qui n'avoit rien veu,
      Fut presque pris au dépourveu.
Voicy comme il conta l'avanture à sa mere.
J'avois franchi les Monts qui bornent cet Etat,
      Et trotois comme un jeune Rat
      Qui cherche à se donner carriere,
Lors que deux animaux m'ont arresté les yeux:
      L'un doux, benin et gracieux,
Et l'autre turbulent, et plein d'inquietude.
      Il a la voix perçante et rude,
      Sur la teste un morceau de chair,
Une sorte de bras dont il s'éleve en l'air
      Comme pour prendre sa volée,
      La queuë en panache étalée.
Or c'estoit un Cochet dont nostre Souriceau
      Fit à sa mere le tableau
Comme d'un animal venu de l'Amerique.
Il se batoit, dit-il, les flancs avec ses bras,
      Faisant tel bruit et tel fracas,
Que moy, qui grace aux Dieux de courage me pique,
      En ay pris la fuite de peur,
      Le maudissant de tres-bon cœur.
      Sans luy j'aurois fait connoissance
Avec cet animal qui m'a semblé si doux.
      Il est velouté comme nous,
Marqueté, longue queue, une humble contenance;
Un modeste regard, et pourtant l'œil luisant:
      Je le crois fort sympatisant
Avec Messieurs les Rats; car il a des oreilles
      En figure aux nôtres pareilles.

The Cockerel, the Cat,
and the Little Mouse

A little mouse—a mouselet, say—had had
    A close escape. Here's how the tad
Explained it to his mother: "Yesterday,
I had just crossed the hills—the ones around
Our state—and I was trotting on my way,
    Just like a strapping ratlet, bound
For foreign climes, when, suddenly, I found
Two animals before me. One looked gracious,
Gentle, and mild; the other seemed pugnacious,
Frightful. Its voice was sharp. It had a bit
Of flesh stuck to its head; and, by its side,
    A funny kind of arm that it
    Flapped up and down, as if it tried
To rise up off the ground. Behind, spread out,
It had a tail." The little mouse, no doubt,
Had seen a cockerel; though, to hear him tell her,
    It might have been some desert dweller
Fresh from America's exotic waste!
    "It flailed and flailed," he said, "and raised
A din that even I—brave, heaven be praised!—
Found terrifying. So I turned and raced
    Back home, cursing the beast. If not
    For him, I'm sure I could have got
To meet the pleasant one. His coat was soft
As ours, with spots; long tail; ears quite a lot
Like rats'… Calm look, bright eyes…" Mother mouse scoffed:
    "You think he likes our kind, that one?
You say that, had the other not begun
His clack and cackle, chasing you away,
    You would have joined him for a chat?

Je l'allois aborder, quand d'un son plein d'éclat
    L'autre m'a fait prendre la fuite.
—Mon fils, dit la Souris, ce doucet est un Chat,
    Qui sous son minois hypocrite
    Contre toute ta parenté
    D'un malin vouloir est porté.
    L'autre animal tout au contraire
    Bien éloigné de nous mal faire,
Servira quelque jour peut-être à nos repas.
Quant au Chat, c'est sur nous qu'il fonde sa cuisine.
    Garde-toy, tant que tu vivras,

Lucky you didn't! That's all I can say!
Sweet though he seems, that hypocrite is Cat!
  His race has vowed, by all the powers,
  Eternal doom on us and ours!
  The other one has no occasion
Ever to prey on those of our persuasion.
Who knows? One day we may, by hook or crook,
  Make him our dinner. But, for Cat,
We are the ones *he* eats, and that is that!
Never, my child, judge folks by how they look!"

VI, 5

Le Chartier Embourbé

Le Phaëton d'une voiture à foin
Vid son char embourbé. Le pauvre homme estoit loin
De tout humain secours. C'estoit à la campagne
Pres d'un certain canton de la basse Bretagne
 Appellé Quimpercorentin.
 On sçait assez que le destin
Adresse là les gens quand il veut qu'on enrage.
 Dieu nous préserve du voyage!
Pour venir au Chartier embourbé dans ces lieux,
Le voila qui deteste et jure de son mieux,
 Pestant en sa fureur extrême
Tantost contre les trous, puis contre ses chevaux,
 Contre son char, contre luy-mesme.
Il invoque à la fin le Dieu dont les travaux
 Sont si celebres dans le monde:

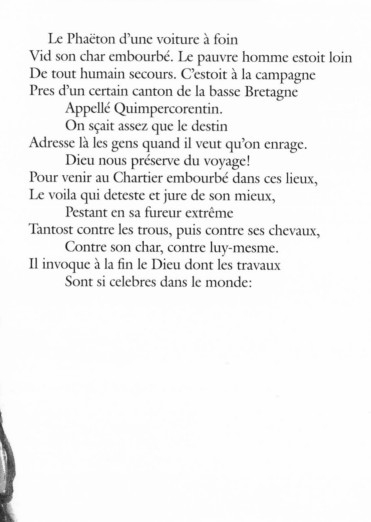

The Wagoner Stuck in the Mud

Carting a load of hay, a peasant
Found that his wagon's wheels were stuck
Fast in the mud, mired in the muck.
To make the mishap all the more unpleasant,
  Monsieur our noble charioteer
Was far from human help; he was, in fact,
  Off in some godforsaken tract
Of Breton wilderness, with nothing near
  But that vile hole, harsh to the ear,
Called Quimpercorentin: [1] harsh to the soul
As well. For there, it seems, Fate leads when she
Would strew our path with wrath and obloquy,
  As we, a-gallop or a-stroll,
Travel about. God spare us!… Now, as for
  The wagoner, bemired, bemucked,
There he stood, ranting: "O ill-starred, ill-lucked!"—
Cursing cart, horses, rut… And, what was more,

Hercule, luy dit-il, aide-moy; si ton dos
      A porté la machine ronde,
      Ton bras peut me tirer d'icy.
Sa priere estant faite, il entend dans la nuë
      Une voix qui lui parle ainsi:
      Hercule veut qu'on se remuë,
Puis il aide les gens. Regarde d'où provient
      L'achopement qui te retient.
      Oste d'autour de chaque rouë
Ce mal-heureux mortier, cette maudite bouë,
      Qui jusqu'à l'aissieu les enduit.
Pren ton pic, et me romps ce caillou qui te nuit.
Comble-moy cette orniere. As-tu-fait? — Oüy, dit l'homme.
— Or bien je vas t'aider, dit la voix: pren ton foüet.
— Je l'ay pris. Qu'est-cecy? mon char marche à souhait.
Hercule en soit loüé. Lors la voix: Tu vois comme
Tes chevaux aisément se sont tirez de là.
      Aide-toy, le Ciel t'aidera.

Cursing himself as well! At length he turned
For succor to that god whose labors earned
His reputation: mighty Hercules.
   "Great god, I beg you hear my prayer,
My supplication! If your back could bear
   Our earthly sphere with utter ease, [2]
Your arm should pull me free!" Next moment, there,
Above his head, out of the clouds, he hears
A voice: "Hercules helps who perseveres.
   Look at the causes of your trouble…
   See? Scrape that mud about the double
Axle betwixt the wheels, sunk deep… That rut?
Fill it!… That stone? The one holding you back?
   Take up your pick and, with a thwack,
Smash it!…" Our friend replies: "It's done. Now what?"
"Now," says the voice, "I'll help you. Take your prod…"
"I've got it… Ah! Look there! Good, gracious god!
My cart… It moves!" The voice: "True, now your horses
Need naught to free them but their own resources."
   The moral? Easy to perceive it:
Heaven helps those who help themselves. Believe it. [3]

VI, 18

113

Le Charlatan

Le monde n'a jamais manqué de Charlatans.
    Cette science de tout temps
    Fut en Professeurs tres-fertile.
Tantost l'un en Theatre affronte l'Acheron,
    Et l'autre affiche par la Ville
    Qu'il est un Passe-Ciceron.
    Un des derniers se vantoit d'estre
    En Eloquence si grand Maistre

The Charlatan

This world, I warrant, never lacks
For charlatans! Call them "imposters," "quacks,"
No matter. Fertile race, they ply their pranks,
Masters at their deceit. Some, mountebanks,
     Well-practiced at those theatre tricks
That—they would have us think—defy the Styx![1]
Some, feigning Ciceronian eloquence,
Would fain surpass the Master! Sheer pretense,

Qu'il rendroit disert un badaut,
Un manant, un rustre, un lourdaut:
Ouy, Messieurs, un lourdaut; un Animal, un Asne.
Que l'on ameine un Asne, un Asne renforcé:
Je le rendray Maistre passé;
Et veux qu'il porte la soutane.
Le Prince sceut la chose; il manda le Rheteur.
J'ay, dit-il, dans mon écurie
Un fort beau Roussin d'Arcadie:
J'en voudrois faire un Orateur.
—Sire, vous pouvez tout, reprit d'abord nôtre homme.
On luy donna certaine somme.
Il devoit au bout de dix ans
Mettre son Asne sur les bancs;
Sinon, il consentoit d'estre en place publique
Guindé la hard au col, étranglé court et net,
Ayant au dos sa Rhetorique
Et les oreilles d'un Baudet.
Quelqu'un des Courtisans luy dit qu'à la potence
Il vouloit l'aller voir, et que, pour un pendu,
Il auroit bonne grace et beaucoup de prestance;
Sur tout qu'il se souvinst de faire à l'assistance
Un discours où son art fut au long étendu,
Un discours pathetique, et dont le formulaire
Servist à certains Cicerons
Vulgairement nommez larrons.
L'autre reprit: Avant l'affaire
Le Roy, l'Asne, ou moy, nous mourrons.

Il avoit raison. C'est folie
De compter sur dix ans de vie.
Soyons bien beuvans, bien mangeans,
Nous devons à la mort de trois l'une en dix ans.

116

Of course; as was the case with one of those
Whom I call "eloquencers." [2] "I propose,"
Said he, "to give the gift of glorious speech
   To some dull lout, some bumptious, crass,
Dumb brute! In fact, messieurs, bring me an ass!
A stupid ass! Not only will I teach
The beast to talk, I'll even have him pass
His doctorate!" [3] His boastings reach the prince's
Ears; and the latter sends for him, evinces
Interest in his art. "I have," says he
   "An ass of finest pedigree, [4]
And wish to make an orator of him."
   "Whatever suits Your Highness' whim,"
Replies our gent. The prince pays him his sum.
"If, in ten years, your royal ass, still dumb,
Speaks not a word, then I agree to stick
A pair of ass ears on my head, and come,
Garroted, with my book of rhetoric
Strapped on my back, to die, hanged, on the square!"
So spoke our quack. One of the courtiers quips:
   "Much would I like to see him there;
   Him and his artful, gracious air,
Pathetic pleadings spouting from his lips!
Eloquent pleadings, in the tone of those
   Common thieves, would-be Ciceros!"
Reasons the fraud: "King, ass, or even I—
   One of us three—is like to die
Before the end, when all is done and said!"

And he was right, for Death demands his due. [5]
Let's eat and drink! In ten years, one or two
Of any three of us might well be dead.

VI, 19

Les Souhaits

Il est au Mogol des folets
Qui font office de valets,
Tiennent la maison propre, ont soin de l'équipage,
Et quelquefois du jardinage.
Si vous touchez à leur ouvrage,
Vous gastez tout. Un d'eux prés du Gange autrefois,
Cultivoit le jardin d'un assez bon Bourgeois.
Il travailloit sans bruit, avoit beaucoup d'adresse,
Aimoit le maistre et la maistresse,
Et le jardin sur tout. Dieu sçait si les zephirs,
Peuple ami du Demon, l'assistoient dans sa tâche.
Le folet de sa part travaillant sans relâche
Combloit ses hostes de plaisirs.
Pour plus de marques de son zele
Chez ces gens pour toûjours il se fust arresté,
Nonobstant la legereté
A ses pareils si naturelle;
Mais ses confreres les esprits
Firent tant que le chef de cette republique,
Par caprice ou par politique,
Le changea bien-tost de logis.
Ordre luy vient d'aller au fond de la Norvege
Prendre le soin d'une maison
En tout temps couverte de neige;
Et d'Indou qu'il estoit on vous le fait lapon.
Avant que de partir, l'esprit dit à ses hostes:
On m'oblige de vous quitter:
Je ne sçais pas pour quelles fautes;
Mais enfin il le faut, je ne puis arrester
Qu'un temps fort court, un mois, peut-estre une semaine.
Employez-la; formez trois souhaits, car je puis

118

The Wishes [1]

Among the Mogols there are genies who
    Serve as valets, clean house—dust, sweep—
Tend to the garden, groom the stables, keep
    The coach in good repair, and do
    Chores of all kinds. But oh! Should you
Lay but a finger on their work, *voilà!*
You spoil it all. Well, years ago there dwelt
Off by the Ganges' shore a good bourgeois,
With such a spirit; one who had been dealt
    Gardening skills galore, and felt
Most kindly toward Monsieur, Madame, and worked
Untiring and without complaint, and not
Unaided by those fair southwinds that lurked
About the garden, breezes wafting hot
(Spirit-companions, they!). Yes, gladly would
Our genie have remained, to toil and moil
With his beloved masters, till the soil
    For them forever, if he could.
    (And that, despite the most capricious
Nature of genies!) But the brotherhood
    Thereof, for reasons—well—suspicious
    (Whimsy? Or politics? Or what?
    Who knows? I have no notion. But…)
The fact is that they changed this one's location:
Off to another corner of the map,
Deep in the wastes of Norway's desolation!
Hindu before, now must he be a Lapp,
And tend a house covered, year-round, with snow!
    "Dear friends," he says, "Before I go—
As go I must, I know not for what sins—
I pray you use the weeks still left to me

Rendre trois souhaits accomplis:
Trois sans plus. Souhaiter, ce n'est pas une peine
        Etrange et nouvelle aux humains.
Ceux-cy pour premier vœu demandent l'abondance,
        Et l'abondance à pleines mains
        Verse en leurs cofres la finance,
En leurs greniers le bled, dans leurs caves les vins;
Tout en creve. Comment ranger cette chevance?
Quels registres, quels soins, quel temps il leur falut!
Tous deux sont empeschez si jamais on le fut.
        Les voleurs contre eux comploterent,
        Les grands Seigneurs leur emprunterent;
Le Prince les taxa. Voilà les pauvres gens
        Malheureux par trop de fortune.
Ostez-nous de ces biens l'affluence importune,
Dirent-ils l'un et l'autre; heureux les indigens!
La pauvreté vaut mieux qu'une telle richesse.
Retirez-vous, tresors, fuyez; et toy, Deesse,
Mere du bon esprit, compagne du repos,
O mediocrité, revien viste. A ces mots,
La mediocrité revient; on luy fait place;
        Avec elle ils rentrent en grace,
Au bout de deux souhaits estant aussi chanceux
        Qu'ils estoient, et que sont tous ceux
Qui souhaitent toûjours et perdent en chimeres
Le temps qu'ils feroient mieux de mettre à leurs affaires.
        Le folet en rit avec eux.
        Pour profiter de sa largesse,
Quand il voulut partir, et qu'il fut sur le poinct,
        Ils demanderent la sagesse:
    C'est un tresor qui n'embarasse point.

To ask me for three wishes. For we jinns,
No doubt you know, can grant Man wishes three—
No less, no more!" Now, wishing, obviously,
Is something Man does well. No need to ask
   Them twice. And, warming to the task:
   "Pray give us wealth!" Such is their first
Request; and wealth they get, but wealth so vast,
In such abundance, that they stand aghast
Before their larder, crammed, ready to burst;
Their cellars, filled with wine, racks upon racks;
Their coffers, stacked with gold! How many the sacks?
Why, who could count it all? Nor had they any
Manner whereby to keep it safe. For many
   The thieves now plotting their attacks;
And many the *grands seigneurs* who, on the morrow,
   Came for their share: beg, steal, or borrow!
(Taxes as well, of course, lest I forget!)
In short, by woe of wealth's excess beset:
   "Misery!" wail our friends. "Please take
Away your treasure and your plenty! Let
   The goddess Poverty come make
Us rich once more, mother of sweet content."
Poverty, at these words returns. Our pair,
At peace again, now with two wishes spent
(Foolishly, but with one yet left), take care
Lest it be wasted on some silly folly.
   Smiling a farewell smile, the jolly
Jinn goes to leave. But our two, with an air
Of melancholy, ask: "If it's your pleasure…
   Our final wish!" And with a touch of
Sadness, they ask for wisdom. Ah, a treasure
No one can ever wish to have too much of!

VII, 5 ^{2}

La Cour du Lion

Sa Majesté Lionne un jour voulut connoistre
De quelles nations le Ciel l'avoit fait maistre.
   Il manda donc par deputez
   Ses vassaux de toute nature,
   Envoyant de tous les costez
   Une circulaire écriture,
   Avec son sceau. L'écrit portoit
   Qu'un mois durant le Roy tiendroit
   Cour pleniere, dont l'ouverture
   Devoit estre un fort grand festin,
   Suivy des tours de Fagotin.
   Par ce trait de magnificence
Le Prince à ses sujets étaloit sa puissance.
   En son Louvre il les invita.
Quel Louvre! un vray charnier, dont l'odeur se porta
D'abord au nez des gens. L'Ours boucha sa narine:
Il se fust bien passé de faire cette mine.
Sa grimace dépleut. Le Monarque irrité
L'envoya chez Pluton faire le dégoûté.
Le Singe approuva fort cette severité,
Et, flateur excessif, il loüa la colere
Et la griffe du Prince, et l'antre, et cette odeur:
   Il n'estoit ambre, il n'estoit fleur,
Qui ne fût ail au prix. Sa sotte flaterie
Eut un mauvais succés, et fut encor punie.
   Ce Monseigneur du Lion là
   Fut parent de Caligula.
Le Renard estant proche: Or çà, luy dit le Sire,
Que sens-tu? dis-le moy. Parle sans déguiser.
   L'autre aussi-tost de s'excuser,
Alleguant un grand rume: il ne pouvoit que dire

King Lion's Court

His Lion Highness, one fine day, decided
Straightway to learn what peoples heaven above
    Had made him sovereign master of,
    And to his deputies confided
    Forthwith the task of sending for
    His vassals: each ambassador
    Bearing a royal-sealed decree
    Declaring that His Majesty
    For one full month was holding court;
    That on the opening day a feast
Would welcome one and all; that ape artiste,
    Famed Fagotin,[1] would then cavort,
    Sporting his monkey tricks. And thus
The monarch, with his lavish, generous
Display would prove his power. All would report
Thence, to his Lion-Louvre, his chateau.
    But as each one alighted, oh!
What a foul stench of death assailed them there!
Holding his nose, contorted, stood Sire Bear.
Our sovereign leonine was much nonplussed
At such a show of disrespect, and he
    Dispatched him most summarily
To Pluto's realm, to practice his disgust.
The monkey, master of the flattering antic,
    Fawning in manner sycophantic,
Finds that the punishment is apt and just; [2]
Praises the prince, his lair… As for the smell,
No flower, no amber could compare! Ah, well,
Lion condemned him too, for toadying!
(A cousin to Caligula, this king!)
    At length, spying the fox: "I say,"
Says he, "tell me, what do you smell? And pray,

Sans odorat; bref il s'en tire.
    Cecy vous sert d'enseignement.
Ne soyez à la Cour, si vous voulez y plaire,
Ny fade adulateur, ny parleur trop sincere;
Et tâchez quelquefois de répondre en Normant.

I'll thank you, friend, for your sake, to be frank!"
Maître Renard, though high His Highness stank,
Replies: "Ah me, I've got a cold, I fear!
What smell?…" Wise beast! To please at court, best you
Be not too honey-tongued nor too sincere:
Answer askew, askance, as Normans do. [3]

VII, 6

L'Homme Qui Court Apres la Fortune, et l'Homme Qui L'Attend dans Son Lit

Qui ne court apres la Fortune?
Je voudrois estre en lieu d'où je pûsse aisément
Contempler la foule importune
De ceux qui cherchent vainement
Cette fille du sort de Royaume en Royaume,
Fideles courtisans d'un volage fantôme.
Quand ils sont prés du bon moment,
L'inconstante aussi-tost à leurs désirs échape;
Pauvres gens, je les plains, car on a pour les fous
Plus de pitié que de courroux.
Cet homme, disent-ils, estoit planteur de choux,
Et le voilà devenu Pape:
Ne le valons-nous pas? Vous valez cent fois mieux:
Mais que vous sert vostre merite?
La Fortune a-t-elle des yeux?
Et puis la papauté vaut-elle ce qu'on quite,
Le repos, le repos, tresor si précieux
Qu'on en faisoit jadis le partage des Dieux?
Rarement la Fortune à ses hostes le laisse.
Ne cherchez point cette Déesse,
Elle vous cherchera: son sexe en use ainsi.
Certain couple d'amis en un bourg étably
Possedoit quelque bien: l'un soûpiroit sans cesse
Pour la Fortune; il dit à l'autre un jour:
Si nous quittions nostre sejour?
Vous sçavez que nul n'est prophete
En son païs. Cherchons nostre avanture ailleurs.
—Cherchez, dit l'autre amy; pour moy, je ne souhaite
Ny climats ny destins meilleurs.
Contentez-vous; suivez votre humeur inquiete:

The Man Who Runs After Fortune, and the Man Who Waits for Her in His Bed

Who doesn't chase Dame Fortune? Ah, how I
Wish I could choose some pleasant place to sit
    And watch her flock of grovelers flit
    Here, there, from realm to realm, and try—
Vain band of sycophantic devotees!—
To find that wanton phantom, Destiny's
    Own daughter! Often, just as they
Approach the fickle wench, she up and flees
    Their lustful grasp! Alackaday!
I pity these poor folk (for surely, one
Should have more pity for the simpleton
    Than wrath!), these fools who say: "But look!
So-and-so was a cabbage planter. Now
They've made him pope![1] Really! And anyhow,
    Where is it written in the book
That I am not as good?" "Oh, but you are!
Better, in fact, a hundred times, by far!
But what of it? Has Fortune eyes to see?
(Besides, as for the papacy, is it
Worth giving up that gift most exquisite—
    The peaceful life, calm, trouble-free—
Dear to the gods themselves; gift that the Beldam
Fortune bestows upon us all too seldom!)
Don't seek the goddess: like her sex, no doubt,
When she wants you, my friend, she'll seek you out."
Two friends there were—a not unwealthy pair—
Who lived together in a certain town.
One of them yearned for Fortune: up and down
He swore to have her: "Come, let us foreswear
This place," said he. "Come, let's be on our way.

Vous reviendrez bien-tost. Je fais vœu cependant
    De dormir en vous attendant.
  L'ambitieux, ou si l'on veut, l'avare,
    S'en va par voye et par chemin.
    Il arriva le lendemain
En un lieu que devoit la Déesse bizarre
Frequenter sur tout autre; et ce lieu, c'est la cour.
Là donc pour quelque-temps il fixe son sejour,
Se trouvant au coucher, au lever, à ces heures
    Que l'on sçait estre les meilleures;
Bref, se trouvant à tout, et n'arrivant à rien.
Qu'est cecy? se dit-il. Cherchons ailleurs du bien.
La Fortune pourtant habite ces demeures.
Je la vois tous les jours entrer chez celuy-cy,
    Chez celuy-là. D'où vient qu'aussi
Je ne puis heberger cette capricieuse?
On me l'avoit bien dit, que des gens de ce lieu
L'on n'aime pas toûjours l'humeur ambitieuse.
Adieu, Messieurs de cour; Messieurs de cour, adieu.
Suivez jusques au bout une ombre qui vous flate.
La Fortune a, dit-on, des temples à Surate;
Allons-là. Ce fut un de dire et s'embarquer.
Ames de bronze, humains, celuy-là fut sans doute
Armé de diamant, qui tenta cette route,
Et le premier osa l'abysme défier.
    Celuy-cy pendant son voyage
    Tourna les yeux vers son village
  Plus d'une fois, essuyant les dangers
Des Pyrates, des vents, du calme, et des rochers,
Ministres de la mort. Avec beaucoup de peines,
On s'en va la chercher en des rives lointaines,

A prophet has no honor, as they say,
    In his own land! So let's go find
Adventure somewhere else!" But, disinclined
To follow him, the other answers: "Nay,
Go ply your quest. Myself, I'll stay behind,
And vow here to remain, asleep, until
Return you shall, for soon return you will." 2
    And so departed our ambitious
Voyager (or ought one say "avaricious"?),
Arriving in a day or two at that
    Especial place, the habitat
Where Fortune, that most curious deity,
Oftenest dwelt; that is, the court. There he
Remained a time, attending when the king
    Rose and retired …3 Alas, in short,
Though he was everywhere, did everything,
    Still, never could he yet consort
With Fortune. "Strange," he thought, "that she comes here
    To lodge with this and that compeer,
But not with me! I've heard the admonition
That those at court abhor too much ambition.
    Methinks such a report is true.
And so, adieu messieurs! Messieurs, adieu!
Pursue your dreams! For me, no doubt Surat, 4
Rich-templed city on the Indies' shore,
Is where Dame Fortune stays most often at.
We'll see!" No sooner said than done. Once more
Our voyager embarks… He who, the first—
Soul of stout bronze—set sail therefor, athirst
For wealth, over the yawning chasm, bore
A heart of diamond! This conquistador,

La trouvant assez tost sans quitter la maison.
L'homme arrive au Mogol; on luy dit qu'au Japon
La Fortune pour lors distribuoit ses graces:
    Il y court; les mers étoient lasses
    De le porter; et tout le fruit
    Qu'il tira de ses longs voyages,

More daunted by the risks—rocks, tempests, calms,
Pirates no less!—now overcome with qualms,
   Thinks more and more of home, yet soon
Reaches the Mogols' realm. But there, Madame's
Minions insist: "If you would have her boon,
Japan is now the most favored of places
Where she bestows—nay, strews!—her generous graces!"
So off he goes… The sea, bored with his whim,
   Having had quite enough of him,

Ce fut cette leçon que donnent les sauvages:
Demeure en ton païs, par la nature instruit.
Le Japon ne fut pas plus heureux à cet homme
    Que le Mogol l'avoit esté;
    Ce qui luy fit conclurre en somme
Qu'il avoit à grand tort son village quité.
    Il renonce aux courses ingrates,
Revient en son païs, void de loin ses pénates,
Pleure de joye, et dit: Heureux qui vit chez soy,
De regler ses desirs faisant tout son employ.
    Il ne sçait que par oüir dire
Çe que c'est que la cour, la mer, et ton empire,
Fortune, qui nous fais passer devant les yeux
Des dignitez, des biens, que jusqu'au bout du monde
On suit sans que l'effet aux promesses réponde.
Desormais je ne bouge, et feray cent fois mieux.
    En raisonnant de cette sorte,
Et contre la Fortune ayant pris ce conseil,
    Il la trouve assise à la porte
De son amy plongé dans un profond sommeil.

Will teach him what the savage knows, to wit:
 Keep to your home and cherish it!
Alas, quite worthless, likewise, was Japan.
"Never should I have ventured, I admit:
Wise now, but what a fool when I began!"
And when, returning whence he came, he sees
 Land, home, and household deities,
 With tears of joy: "Happy the man,"
He cries, "who stays close by his hearth, each day
Cooling that foolish passion that would surely
 Carry him off, lead him astray!
Better to listen, safely and securely,
To tales of court, seas, and the whole array
That Fortune dangles, rich, before our eyes,
Rather than seek them in a futile race
Spanning the earth! No more the merry chase
For me!..." As thus he moans, and sighs his sighs,
Reviling Fortune's evils without number,
He finds her sitting at his friend's front door,
 And him, whom he had left before,
Still sleeping in his bed, deep in his slumber.

VII, II [5]

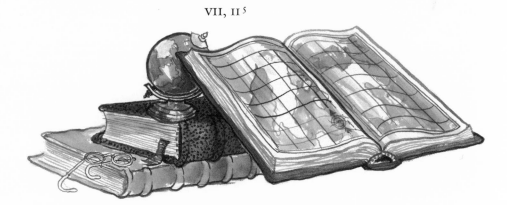

Le Chat, la Belette,
et le Petit Lapin

Du palais d'un jeune Lapin
Dame Belette un beau matin
S'empara: c'est une rusée.
Le Maistre estant absent, ce luy fut chose aisée.
Elle porta chez luy ses pénates un jour
Qu'il estoit allé faire à l'Aurore sa cour
Parmy le thim et la rosée.
Aprés qu'il eut brouté, troté, fait tous ses tours,
Janot Lapin retourne aux soûterrains sejours.
La Belette avoit mis le nez à la fenestre.
O Dieux hospitaliers, que vois-je icy paroistre?
Dit l'animal chassé du paternel logis.
O là! Madame la Belette,
Que l'on déloge sans trompette,
Ou je vais avertir tous les rats du païs.
La Dame au nez pointu répondit que la terre
Estoit au premier occupant.
C'estoit un beau sujet de guerre
Qu'un logis où luy-mesme il n'entroit qu'en rampant.
Et quand ce seroit un Royaume,
Je voudrois bien sçavoir, dit-elle, quelle loy
En a pour toûjours fait l'octroy
A Jean, fils ou nepveu de Pierre ou de Guillaume,
Plutost qu'à Paul, plutost qu'à moy.
Jean Lapin allegua la coustume et l'usage.
Ce sont, dit-il, leurs loix qui m'ont de ce logis
Rendu maistre et seigneur, et qui, de pere en fils,
L'ont de Pierre à Simon, puis à moy Jean transmis.
Le premier ocupant, est-ce une loy plus sage?
—Or bien, sans crier davantage,
Rapportons-nous, dit-elle, à Raminagrobis.
C'estoit un chat vivant comme un dévot hermite,

The Cat, the Weasel, and the Little Rabbit

One morning, not without a certain malice,
   Dame Weasel—she of ruse and guile—
   Invaded a young rabbit's palace.
The master of the manor, all the while,
   Was off amid the thyme and dew
Paying the Dawn his court (a *rendez-vous*
   D'amour!), and it was with great ease
   That weasel came and settled in,
Installed her own household divinities.
Rabbit—once he had turned his cap-a-pie's,
   Nibbled, taken his morning spin—
Bounds to his underground domain; therein
Sees weasel at the window, snout protruding.
"Ye gods of the ancestral roof! What's this
   I see? I fear much is amiss!"
   Cries the evicted host, concluding:
"Out, Madame Weasel, and be quick about it!
   If not, I'll send for rats from far
And near! And then, my dear, it's *au revoir!*"
She of the meager muzzle sneers: "I doubt it.
The land belongs to those who took it first.
   Strange cause for war between us, when
It wasn't yours to start with even then!"
And on and on, with logic, she rehearsed
Her argument. "And even if this were
A kingdom, I should like to know, monsieur,
   What law, in perpetuity,
Bequeathed it to your kind and not to me!
Why Jean, the son or nephew of Guillaume,
   Or of Pierre? Why rabbits all,
I ask, and not, perhaps, say, one named 'Paul'?"
"Custom," Jean answered, "made this place our home,
   Father to son, each generation."
Weasel suggests: "Why must we squabble more?

Un chat faisant la chatemite,
Un saint homme de chat, bien fourré, gros et gras,
Arbitre expert sur tous les cas.
Jean Lapin pour juge l'agrée.
Les voila tous deux arrivez
Devant sa majesté fourrée.
Grippeminaud leur dit: Mes enfans, approchez,
Approchez; je suis sourd; les ans en sont la cause.
L'un et l'autre approcha, ne craignant nulle chose.
Aussi-tost qu'à portée il vid les contestans,
Grippeminaud le bon apostre,
Jettant des deux costez la griffe en mesme temps,
Mit les plaideurs d'accord en croquant l'un et l'autre.
Ceci ressemble fort aux debats qu'ont par fois
Les petits souverains se rapportans aux Rois.

Rather let's take our case before
The saintly Friar Cat for arbitration."
One of Raminagrobis' clan,[1] said cat—
    Ascetic, sleek, fat, and well-furred,
    Well-versed in law—frequently heard
Such litigation. Jean agrees. Thereat
They both approach the holy habitat
Of His Grimalkinship. "Come closer, please,
My children. Else," says he, "I cannot hear.
I'm deaf. Old age has wrought infirmities
Galore upon me!" So the pair draw near.
When thus he sees both well within his reach,
Our pharisee whips out a claw at each,
    And, with a look of saintly cheer,
Solves their complaint with but a pair of swallows.
    From which, perhaps, you'll find it follows
That petty princes, if they be astute,
Should not ask kings to settle their dispute.

VII, I5

Le Savetier et le Financier

Un Savetier chantoit du matin jusqu'au soir:
C'estoit merveilles de le voir,
Merveilles de l'oüir; il faisoit des passages,
Plus content qu'aucun des sept sages.
Son voisin au contraire, estant tout cousu d'or,
Chantoit peu, dormoit moins encor.
C'estoit un homme de finance.
Si sur le poinct du jour parfois il sommeilloit,
Le Savetier alors en chantant l'éveilloit,
Et le Financier se plaignoit
Que les soins de la Providence
N'eussent pas au marché fait vendre le dormir
Comme le manger et le boire.
En son hostel il fait venir
Le chanteur, et luy dit: Or ça, sire Gregoire,
Que gagnez-vous par an? —Par an? Ma foy, Monsieur,
Dit avec un ton de rieur
Le gaillard Savetier, ce n'est point ma maniere

The Cobbler and the Financier

A cobbler used to sing from morn till night.
    It was, indeed, a wondrous thing
To watch him, hear him warble with delight,
    Happier in his laboring
Than any of the Seven Sages were. [1]
Close by, a neighbor—quite the fine *monsieur*,
Rich as a king!—sang little, slept still less.
    He was, in fact (as you might guess),
    The kind we dub a "financier."
When, at the break of dawn, he dozed a bit,
    All of a sudden he would hear
    The cobbler's joyous song, and it
Would rouse him. "Ha," he grumbled, "why oh why
Has it not been ordained that we might buy
    Our sleep as we buy food and drink!"
He calls the singer to his habitat.
"What do you earn each year?" he asks. Whereat
Grégoire replies, laughing, and with a wink:
"A year? Monsieur, I fear that's not my way

139

De compter de la sorte, et je n'entasse guere
    Un jour sur l'autre: il suffit qu'à la fin
        J'attrape le bout de l'année.
        Chaque jour amene son pain.
—Et bien! que gagnez-vous, dites-moy, par journée?
—Tantost plus, tantost moins: le mal est que toûjours,
(Et sans cela nos gains seroient assez honnestes,)
Le mal est que dans l'an s'entremeslent des jours
    Qu'il faut chommer: on nous ruine en Festes.
L'une fait tort à l'autre, et Monsieur le Curé
De quelque nouveau Saint charge toûjours son prône.
Le Financier, riant de sa naïveté,
Luy dit: Je vous veux mettre aujourd'huy sur le trône.
Prenez ces cent écus: gardez les avec soin,
    Pour vous en servir au besoin.
Le Savetier crut voir tout l'argent que la terre
        Avoit depuis plus de cent ans
        Produit pour l'usage des gens.
Il retourne chez luy; dans sa cave il enserre
        L'argent et sa joye à la fois.
        Plus de chant; il perdit la voix
Du moment qu'il gagna ce qui cause nos peines.
        Le sommeil quitta son logis,
        Il eut pour hostes les soucis,
        Les soupçons, les alarmes vaines.
Tout le jour il avoit l'œil au guet. Et la nuit,
        Si quelque chat faisoit du bruit,
Le chat prenoit l'argent. A la fin le pauvre homme
S'en courut chez celuy qu'il ne réveilloit plus.
Rendez-moy, luy dit-il, mes chansons et mon somme,
        Et reprenez vos cent écus.

Of figuring! I'm happy, day by day,
    To do my tasks and, by year's end,
    Make both ends meet!" "Well then, my friend,
What do you earn each day?" "That's hard to say.
Some more, some less… The problem—and it surely
Is one: without it, I would do just fine!—
The problem is that sometimes I do poorly,
What with these blessèd holidays of mine,
Each time the priest finds some new saint to fete!"
Laughing at his simplicity, his host
    Offers a most untoward riposte:
    "My friend, today you can forget
    Your problems, bid them *au revoir!*
Here are a hundred crown! Save them, and let
Them serve you well in time of need!" Grégoire
    Gapes at the sum and thinks he sees
    All of the coins that centuries
    Had struck for mankind's use! Posthaste
    He took his leave, quick as you please,
And raced back to his hovel. There, he placed
His fortune underground, deep in the earth.
Alas, there with his wealth went all his mirth!
    No more, now, will he sing. No more
Has he the joyous voice he had before;
For now his are the cares that fortune brings.
    No more his peaceful slumberings:
By day, on guard against some predator;
By night, alarmed each time the cat would make
A sound, convinced a thief had come to break
    Into his horde! At length he flies
Off to Monsieur—unwakened now!—and, flinging
    The hundred crown before him, cries:
"Here! Take them! Just give back my sleep, my singing!"

VIII, 2

141

Les Femmes et le Secret

Rien ne pese tant qu'un secret;
Le porter loin est difficile aux Dames;
Et je sçais mesme sur ce fait
Bon nombre d'hommes qui sont femmes.
Pour éprouver la sienne un mari s'écria
La nuit estant prés d'elle: O dieux! qu'est-ce cela?
Je n'en puis plus; on me déchire;
Quoy! j'accouche d'un œuf!—D'un œuf?—Oüy, le voilà,

Women and Secrets [1]

Nothing there is that weighs so heavily
As someone's secret. Women, more than men,
Find it impossible to bear. (But then,
    If truth be told, I guarantee,
    Many's the man who, though a "he,"
    Acts like a "she" in this regard!)
To put his woman to the test, a man,
One night, lying beside his mate, began
To yelp in pain: "Ah, help!... O fate ill-starred!
    What's this?... I... Oh! Ye gods! I've laid

Frais et nouveau pondu: gardez bien de le dire:
On m'appelleroit poule. Enfin n'en parlez pas.
  La femme neuve sur ce cas,
  Ainsi que sur mainte autre affaire,
Crut la chose, et promit ses grands dieux de se taire.
  Mais ce serment s'évanoüit
  Avec les ombres de la nuit.
  L'épouse indiscrete et peu fine
Sort du lit quand le jour fut à peine levé;
  Et de courir chez sa voisine.
Ma commere, dit-elle, un cas est arrivé.
N'en dites rien sur tout, car vous me feriez battre.
Mon mary vient de pondre un œuf gros comme quatre.
  Au nom de Dieu, gardez-vous bien
  D'aller publier ce mystere.
—Vous moquez-vous? dit l'autre. Ah, vous ne sçavez guere
  Quelle je suis. Allez, ne craignez rien.
La femme du pondeur s'en retourne chez elle.
L'autre grille déja de conter la nouvelle:
Elle va la répandre en plus de dix endroits.
  Au lieu d'un œuf elle en dit trois.
Ce n'est pas encor tout, car une autre commere
En dit quatre, et raconte à l'oreille le fait;
  Precaution peu necessaire,
  Car ce n'estoit plus un secret.
Comme le nombre d'œufs, grace à la renommée,
  De bouche en bouche alloit croissant,
  Avant la fin de la journée
  Il se montoient à plus d'un cent.

An egg!" "An egg?" queried the wife. "Just so!"
Replied the man. "A fine, fresh egg! But oh!
    Please keep my secret! I'm afraid
Lest people jeer and tell me I'm a hen!"
    Naïve, to say the least, the wife
Believed him, swore upon her very life
    Never to breathe a word. But when
    Daylight has dawned, her resolution
Pales with the fading shades of night; and then—
    True to her female constitution—
    She jumps from bed and promptly hies her
    Straight to her neighbor, to apprise her.
"*Commère,* you can't imagine what befell! You
    Never will guess… Well, let me tell you.
Only, however, if you promise not
To tell a soul, or I'll be beaten!… Well, you
Never… My husband laid an egg!" "He what?"
    "Yes, and a big one! But I beg
You not tell anyone!" "How can you doubt me?
I can keep secrets! That's one thing about me!"
Whereat the wife of him who laid the egg
Went home. The other, though, yearns, burns to spread
    The news; and so goes here, goes there,
    Into a dozen houses, where
    The story grows. Because, instead
    Of just one egg, she tells of three.
    Nor was that all: another made
It four, in fact. (Still in a whisper, she—
    Though now, no matter, I'm afraid:
The secret was no more!) And on and on,
Until our layer—O phenomenon!—
By day's end, lo! a hundred eggs had laid.

VIII, 6

145

Le Rieur et les Poissons

On cherche les Rieurs, et moy, je les évite.
Cet art veut sur tout autre un suprême merite.
    Dieu ne crea que pour les sots
    Les méchans diseurs de bons mots.
    J'en vais peut-estre en une Fable
    Introduire un; peut-estre aussi
Que quelqu'un trouvera que j'auray reussi.
    Un rieur estoit à la table
   D'un Financier, et n'avoit en son coin
Que de petits poissons; tous les gros estoient loin.
Il prend donc les menus, puis leur parle à l'oreille,
    Et puis il feint, à la pareille,
D'écouter leur réponse. On demeura surpris;
    Cela suspendit les esprits.
    Le Rieur alors d'un ton sage
    Dit qu'il craignoit qu'un sien amy,
    Pour les grandes Indes party,
    N'eust depuis un an fait naufrage.
Il s'en informoit donc à ce menu fretin;
Mais tous luy répondoient qu'ils n'étoient pas d'un âge
    A sçavoir au vray son destin;
    Les gros en sçauroient davantage.
N'en puis-je donc, Messieurs, un gros interroger?
    De dire si la compagnie
    Prit goust à sa plaisanterie,
J'en doute; mais enfin, il les sceut engager
A luy servir d'un monstre assez vieux pour luy dire
Tous les noms des chercheurs de mondes inconnus
    Qui n'en estoient pas revenus,
Et que depuis cent ans sous l'abysme avoient veus
    Les anciens du vaste empire.

The Joker and the Fish

Some folk seek out the company of jokers.
    Myself, I shun these laugh-provokers'
    Ilk: those who think their silly wit
    Transcends all art, though surely it
Falls short! For fools has God created those
Pun-makers, bad *bon mot* magnificos.
Now, in a fable, I shall try to fit
My wit to theirs: we'll see if I am able.
A financier was playing host, at table,
To dinner guests. Among the latter sat
    One of our jokesters, on whose platter
Lay but a few small, meager fish. The fatter,
Larger ones lay on others' plates; whereat
    Monsieur the wag holds up his dish,
And, with his lips pressed to the scrawny fish,
He feigns to whisper something in their ears;
Then, listening in turn, pretends he hears
Their answer. Clearly there was much surprise.
    Thus, in his most mock-serious wise,
    And with a sham-tormented frown,
Says he: "I asked if they had any news
About a friend bound for the Indies, whose
    Vessel, I fear, might have gone down.
'We're much too young to know,' they said. 'Our bigger
Relatives would know better.' So, I figure,
Perhaps, if messieurs would be kind enough
To give me one, I'll ask." Funny or not,
I don't know how they took it. But he got
    His fish: a big one, but so tough,
So old that it could easily have named
Every explorer seeking worlds uncharted
For the last hundred years; those long departed
Souls that the seas' vast, ancient wastes had claimed!

VIII, 8

Le Rat et l'Huitre

Un Rat hoste d'un champ, Rat de peu de cervelle,
Des Lares paternels un jour se trouva sou.
Il laisse-là le champ, le grain, et la javelle,
Va courir le païs, abandonne son trou.
        Si-tost qu'il fut hors de la case:
Que le monde, dit-il, est grand et spacieux!
Voilà les Apennins, et voicy le Caucase.
La moindre Taupinée étoit mont à ses yeux.
Au bout de quelques jours le voyageur arrive
En un certain canton où Thetis sur la rive
Avoit laissé mainte Huitre; et nostre Rat d'abord
Crût voir en les voyant des vaisseaux de haut bord.
Certes, dit-il, mon pere estoit un pauvre sire:
Il n'osoit voyager, craintif au dernier point:

The Rat and the Oyster

A country rat—a beast of little wit—
Glutted on rustic life, decides to quit
    The hearth paternal; and he leaves
    His hole, the field, the golden sheaves
    Of grain, to roam the country round.
No sooner has he left his home than he
Is startled by such vast immensity!
    "How big this world! Why, I'll be bound,
Here are the Apennines... The Caucasus..."
    For him the merest molehill mound
Was a huge mount. And so his exodus
Continues, till, a few days hence, he reaches
    One of the goddess Tethys' beaches, [1]
A shore where she had laid, in grand profusion,
    Many an oyster; whence our rat
    Was quick to come to the conclusion

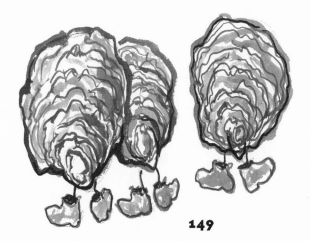

Pour moy, j'ay déja veu le maritime empire;
J'ay passé les deserts, mais nous n'y bûmes point.
D'un certain magister le Rat tenoit ces choses,
        Et les disoit à travers champs,
N'estant pas de ces Rats qui les livres rongeans
        Se font sçavans jusques aux dents.
        Parmy tant d'Huitres toutes closes,
Une s'estoit ouverte, et bâillant au Soleil,
        Par un doux Zephir réjoüie,
Humoit l'air, respiroit, estoit épanoüie,
Blanche, grasse, et d'un goust à la voir nompareil.
D'aussi loin que le Rat voit cette Huitre qui bâille:
Qu'apperçois-je? dit-il, c'est quelque victuaille;
Et si je ne me trompe à la couleur du mets,
Je dois faire aujourd'huy bonne chere, ou jamais.
Là-dessus maistre Rat, plein de belle esperance,
Approche de l'écaille, allonge un peu le cou,
Se sent pris comme aux lacs: car l'Huitre tout d'un coup
Se referme, et voilà ce que fait l'ignorance.

Cette Fable contient plus d'un enseignement.
        Nous y voyons premierement
Que ceux qui n'ont du monde aucune experience
Sont aux moindres objets frappez d'étonnement;
        Et puis nous y pouvons apprendre
        Que tel est pris qui croyoit prendre.

That these were oceangoing craft; whereat:
"My father," he reflected, "was a poor,
    Timid old soul, who, to be sure,
Never once ventured from his hole to seek
His fortune, unlike me! No mousey, meek
Creature am I! I've seen the seas' expanse,
The deserts' too, without a drop to drink!"
    And on he rants, citing, I think,
Some learnèd *magister* whom he, by chance,
    Had heard somewhere. For he, in truth,
Was not one of your rats of eager tooth
Who gnaw on books and grow in wisdom!... Well,
At length one of the oysters, spread pell-mell,
Opens... Yawns at the sun... Sniffs the fair breeze:
    Plump, white of flesh, and seeming quite
    The tender morsel. "No boats these," [2]
Cries rat! "I think I'll have myself a bite!"
He tried... Approached... Bit... But the oyster, snapping,
    Trapping our traveler, caught him napping:
Shells that can open can, as quickly, close!

Two things this fable teaches: first, that those
With little knowledge of the world will be
    Awed by its slightest novelty;
    Second, that—as the maxim goes—
When ill-intentioned, best we be on guard
Lest we be hoist upon our own petard! [3]

                       VIII, 9

L'Asne et le Chien

Il se faut entr'ayder; c'est la loy de nature.
    L'Asne un jour pourtant s'en moqua:
    Et ne sçais comme il y manqua;
    Car il est bonne creature.
Il alloit par pays accompagné du Chien,
    Gravement, sans songer à rien,
    Tous deux suivis d'un commun maître.
Ce maistre s'endormit: l'Asne se mit à paître.
    Il estoit alors dans un pré,
    Dont l'herbe estoit fort à son gré.
Point de chardons pourtant; il s'en passa pour l'heure:
Il ne faut pas toûjours estre si délicat;
    Et faute de servir ce plat
    Rarement un festin demeure.
    Nostre Baudet s'en sceut enfin
Passer pour cette fois. Le Chien mourant de faim
Luy dit: Cher compagnon, baisse-toy, je te prie;
Je prendray mon disné dans le panier au pain.
Point de réponse, mot: le Roussin d'Arcadie
    Craignit qu'en perdant un moment
    Il ne perdist un coup de dent.
    Il fit long-temps la sourde oreille.
Enfin il répondit: Amy, je te conseille
D'attendre que ton maistre ait fini son sommeil,
Car il te donnera sans faute à son réveil

The Ass and the Dog

We must help one another; yea, it
Verily is a law of Nature. But
   An ass, one day, failed to obey it.
   Why? Who can say? I don't know what
   The reason might have been, because
He was a worthy sort. Well, there he was,
That day, he and a dog, wending their way
   Without a single thought in mind,
And with their master coming up behind.
   The latter, suddenly, as they
Trod loping on, fell fast asleep. And so
The ass began to graze the grass, abounding
   Over the pastureland, surrounding,
   Feasting his heart's content, although
   There were no prickly thorns—the kind
   That feast must have for ass to find
It to his liking!… Anyway, no need
To be so fussy. There he was, with feed
   A-plenty, even though it lacked
   Perfection!… Now, the dog, in fact,
Lay almost dead from hunger, and he said:
"Dear friend, I beg you, please, lower your head
And let me take my dinner in that basket
Hanging about your neck." Sire Quadruped, [1]
Though many a time the dog again would ask it,
   Turned a deaf ear, a-chomping, lest
He lose a bite. At last: "Friend, I suggest,"
He answered, "that you wait until Monsieur

153

Ta portion accoûtumée.
Il ne sçauroit tarder beaucoup.
Sur ces entrefaites un Loup
Sort du bois, et s'en vient; autre beste affamée.
L'Asne appelle aussi-tost le Chien à son secours.
Le Chien ne bouge, et dit: Amy, je te conseille
De fuir en attendant que ton maistre s'éveille:
Il ne sçauroit tarder; détale viste, et cours,
Que si ce Loup t'atteint, casse-luy la machoire.
On t'a ferré de neuf; et si tu me veux croire,
Tu l'étendras tout plat. Pendant ce beau discours,
Seigneur Loup étrangla le Baudet sans remede.
Je conclus qu'il faut qu'on s'entr'ayde.

Awakes. He'll not be long… He'll not demur,
But will give you your due." As he addressed
Him thus, a wolf came at them from the wood.
Another hungry beast! The ass turned toward
    The dog: "Help! Help me!" he implored.
    But, unafraid, the latter stood
    His ground. "Friend, were I you, I should
Run off! Monsieur will wake… He'll not be long…
    Still, better you not hem and haw.
    Now, if you're caught, you won't go wrong
Using your new-shod hooves to break a jaw,
    And lay him flat…" During said song
And dance, Sire Wolf strangled our ass, quite dead.
Yes, best we help each other, as I've said.

VIII, 17

155

Le Chat et le Rat

Quatre animaux divers, le Chat grippe-fromage,
Triste-oiseau le Hibou, Ronge-maille le Rat,
    Dame Belette au long corsage,
    Toutes gens d'esprit scelerat,
Hantoient le tronc pourry d'un pin vieux et sauvage.
Tant y furent qu'un soir à l'entour de ce pin
L'homme tendit ses rets. Le Chat de grand matin
    Sort pour aller chercher sa proye.
Les derniers traits de l'ombre empeschent qu'il ne voye
Le filet; il y tombe, en danger de mourir:
Et mon Chat de crier, et le Rat d'accourir,
L'un plein de desespoir, et l'autre plein de joye:
Il voyoit dans les las son mortel ennemy.
    Le pauvre Chat dit: Cher amy,
    Les marques de ta bienveillance
    Sont communes en mon endroit:
Vien m'aider à sortir du piege où l'ignorance
    M'a fait tomber. C'est à bon droit
Que seul entre les tiens par amour singuliere
Je t'ay toujours choyé, t'aimant comme mes yeux.
Je n'en ay point regret, et j'en rends grace aux Dieux.
    J'allois leur faire ma priere,
Comme tout devot Chat en use les matins.
Ce rezeau me retient; ma vie est en tes mains:

The Cat and the Rat

Four animals—Nip-Cheese the cat,
  Sad-Bird the owl, Gnaw-Stitch the rat,
And Madame Weasel, of the lithe, sleek breast,
  Each one especially unblest
With nasty temperament—all lived inside
A rotting, old, wild pinetree's trunk. One night
A man approached their dwelling and spread wide
His snares about the tree. Next morning, bright
And early—as her wont—the cat arises,
Goes out to seek his prey… Now, one surmises
That, in the breaking dawn's still dusky light,
He fails to see the net, and in he falls…
  Wailing his woe, he squeals, he calls,
Lest, there ensnared, he languish, end his days.
  The rat comes running out, surveys
The situation, overjoyed to see
  Nip-Cheese, his mortal enemy,
  Properly tangled in the snare.
Laments the poor cat: "Ah, Gnaw-Stitch, *mon cher,*
You, who have ever been so good to me,
Come save me from this agony that my
Stupidity alone has caused! I pray you,
  Come, you, the apple of my eye!
  My life is in your paws! What say you?
You, whom, of all your kind, alone I love!
Why, just now I was on my way to say
  My prayers! For, by the gods above,

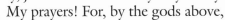

Vien dissoudre ces nœuds.—Et quelle recompense
    En auray-je? reprit le Rat.
      —Je jure eternelle alliance
    Avec toy, repartit le Chat.
Dispose de ma griffe, et sois en assurance:
Envers et contre tous je te protegeray,
    Et la Belette mangeray,
    Avec l'époux de la Choüette.
Ils t'en veulent tous deux. Le Rat dit: Idiot!
Moy, ton liberateur? Je ne suis pas si sot.
    Puis il s'en va vers sa retraite.
    La Belette, estoit prés du trou.
Le Rat grimpe plus haut: il y void le Hibou:
Dangers de toutes parts; le plus pressant l'emporte.
Ronge-maille retourne au Chat, et fait en sorte
Qu'il détache un chaisnon, puis un autre, et puis tant
    Qu'il dégage enfin l'hypocrite.
    L'homme paroist en cet instant.
Les nouveaux alliez prennent tous deux la fuite.
A quelque-temps delà, nostre Chat vid de loin
Son Rat qui se tenoit à l'erte et sur ses gardes.
Ah! mon frere, dit-il, vien m'embrasser; ton soin
    Me fait injure. Tu regardes
    Comme ennemy ton allié.
    Penses-tu que j'aye oublié
    Qu'apres Dieu je te dois la vie?
—Et moy, reprit le Rat, penses-tu que j'oublie
    Ton naturel? Aucun traité
Peut-il forcer un Chat à la reconnoissance?
    S'assure-t-on sur l'alliance
    Qu'a faite la necessité?

A pious cat am I, and every day
I pray for you! Now, be a dear and come
Nibble this net and end my martyrdom!"
    "Oh?" says the rat. "And, if I gnaw
You free, what will you do for me?" "'Do'? Why,
I swear ever to be your staunch ally,
Against your enemies, with tooth and claw!
Weasel and owl will I devour, for they
    Wish you much ill! Now, *s'il vous plaît...*"
    The rat replies with a guffaw:
"What kind of fool...! Me, save your hide? How droll!"
    And off he scurries to his hole,
Only to find the weasel lurking there.
So up the tree he hurries... But, despair!
There sits the owl! What can he do? Thereat,
Attending to the pressing problem first,
    Back he goes trotting to the cat,
Gnaws at the net... Here, there... The stitches burst,
    And Nip-Cheese, wily pharisee,
Breaks free! But, at that moment, suddenly,
The man approaches, and our new allies
Take to their heels... Time passes. Then, one day,
    The cat, off in the distance, spies
The rat; the latter darts his wary eyes
Around, about... The former beckons: "Pray,
Brother mine! Come give me a hug! I'm much
Distressed to see you eye your friend with such
Distrust! Can you suppose that I forget
That it was you who saved me from the net?
Why, after God, I owe my life to you!"
"And you," rat answered, "do you think I yet
Forget your nature? Nay, it's all too true:
    You're still a cat! Who can rely
On friendship born of need? My friend, not I!"

VIII, 22

Les Deux Chiens et l'Asne Mort

Les vertus devroient estre sœurs,
Ainsi que les vices sont freres:
Dés que l'un de ceux-cy s'empare de nos cœurs,
Tous viennent à la file, il ne s'en manque gueres;
J'entends de ceux qui n'estant pas contraires
Peuvent loger sous mesme toit.
A l'égard des vertus, rarement on les void
Toutes en un sujet eminemment placées,
Se tenir par la main sans estre dispersées.
L'un est vaillant, mais prompt; l'autre est prudent, mais froid.
Parmy les animaux, le Chien se pique d'être
Soigneux et fidele à son maistre;
Mais il est sot, il est gourmand:
Témoin ces deux mâtins qui dans l'éloignement

The Two Dogs and the Dead Ass

Virtues are sisters, I suppose;
And vices, brothers. For, when one of those—
Vices, I mean—lays hold upon our hearts,
The others follow: it was ever thus.
(So long as each, that is, without a fuss,
   Can live amongst his counterparts
Under one roof.) It's not the same at all
With virtues. No, seldom does it befall
   That all of them are seen to mingle
   Peaceably, lodging in a single
Creature, united hand in hand withal.
   One may be valiant, brave, and daring,
But lack reflection; and we may observe
Another, wise and cautious, but uncaring,
   Callous, and cold. The dog will serve
As good example. Faithful to a fault,

Virent un Asne mort qui flotoit sur les ondes.
Le vent de plus en plus l'éloignoit de nos Chiens.
Amy, dit l'un, tes yeux sont meilleurs que les miens.
Porte un peu tes regards sur ces plaines profondes.
J'y crois voir quelque chose. Est-ce un Bœuf? un Cheval?
      —Hé! qu'importe quel animal?
Dit l'un de ces mastins; voila toujours curée.
Le point est de l'avoir: car le trajet est grand;
Et de plus il nous faut nager contre le vent.
Beuvons toute cette eau: nostre gorge alterée
En viendra bien à bout: ce corps demeurera
      Bien-tost à sec, et ce sera
      Provision pour la semaine.
Voila mes Chiens à boire; ils perdirent l'haleine,
      Et puis la vie; ils firent tant
      Qu'on les vid crever à instant.
L'homme est ainsi basti. Quand un sujet l'enflâme,
L'impossibilité disparoist à son ame.
Combien fait-il de vœux, combien perd-il de pas,
S'outrant pour acquerir des biens ou de la gloire?
      Si j'arrondissois mes estats!
Si je pouvois remplir mes coffres de ducats!
Si j'apprenois l'hebreu, les sciences, l'histoire!
      Tout cela, c'est la mer à boire;
      Mais rien à l'homme ne suffit:
Pour fournir aux projets que forme un seul esprit
Il faudroit quatre corps; encor loin d'y suffire
A my chemin je crois que tous demeureroient:
Quatre Mathusalems bout à bout ne pourroient
      Mettre à fin ce qu'un seul desire.

It's he, of all the beasts, whom we exalt
    Above the rest. Yet weak of wit
He is, and much too strong of appetite.
    Witness—should you need proof of it—
A pair of hounds who, one fair day, caught sight,
Off in the distance, of a dead ass floating
    Over the waves, and, likewise, noting
That it was being blown out to sea. "Your eyes,"
    Said one, "are much more powerful
Than mine. See, there? Is that a horse or bull?"
"What difference?" said the other. "It's a prize,
    Whichever! Both are meat! Let's glut!
    It's a long swim, and windward; but
    Let's drink: our throats, parched dry, will make
Short order of the sea. Then, once we slake
Our thirst, that hunk will serve for many a day."
And so they drink; and, having drunk, at first
They lose their breath… And then their life: they burst.
So too with Man: when passion comes his way
And lights a fire, his mind and soul reject
    The notion that he cannot reach
His goal. He strives, he fights: to no effect!
Too vast the ocean! Power, possessions… Each
Becomes desire. "If only I might learn:
History, Hebrew, science! Ah, I burn
To understand!" But no, one life, for Man,
Is not enough. He yearns to drink the sea!
    Even four times as long, his span
Would not be half as much as it should be!
And four Methuselahs, laid tip to toe,
Never could learn what mankind yearns to know. [1]

VIII, 25

L'Huitre et les Plaideurs

Un jour deux Pelerins sur le sable rencontrent
Une Huitre que le flot y venoit d'apporter:
Ils l'avalent des yeux, du doigt ils se la montrent;
A l'égard de la dent, il falut contester.
L'un se baissoit déja pour amasser la proye;
L'autre le pousse, et dit: Il est bon de sçavoir
      Qui de nous en aura la joye.
Celuy qui le premier a pû l'appercevoir
En sera le gobeur; l'autre le verra faire.
     —Si par-là l'on juge l'affaire,
Reprit son compagnon, j'ay l'œil bon, Dieu mercy.
     —Je ne l'ay pas mauvais aussi,
Dit l'autre, et je l'ay veuë avant vous sur ma vie.
—Et bien, vous l'avez veuë, et moy je l'ay sentie.
     Pendant tout ce bel incident,
Perrin Dandin arrive: ils le prennent pour juge.
Perrin fort gravement ouvre l'Huitre, et la gruge,
     Nos deux Messieurs le regardant.
Ce repas fait, il dit d'un ton de President:
Tenez, la Cour vous donne à chacun une écaille,
Sans dépens, et qu'en paix chacun chez soi s'en aille.
Mettez ce qu'il en coûte à plaider aujourd'huy;
Comptez ce qu'il en reste à beaucoup de familles;
Vous verrez que Perrin tire l'argent à luy,
Et ne laisse aux plaideurs que le sac et les quilles.

The Oyster and the Adversaries

A pair of pilgrims, on a sandy beach,
Happen upon an oyster, which the tide
Had just washed in and laid before them. Each
Gobbles it with his glance, covetous-eyed,
Waggles a finger. But, as for the right
Of tooth, forsooth—or, so to speak, of bite—
Ah, that will be the cause of hot debate.
　　Already one of them is bending
　　Low to pick up the prize, when: "Wait,
　　My friend," the other cries, contending.
　　And, with a shove: "The one who saw it
First gets to gulp that dish! The other need
　　But watch!" His friend replies: "Agreed!
It's mine! My sight, thank God, is perfect!" "Pshaw! It
Isn't as fine as mine! I saw it first!"
"Perhaps, but me, I smelled it long before!…"
　　As thus they quibbled, carped, conversed,
Pierre the peasant[1] lopes along the shore.
"Come, be the judge," they say. With that, the lout
Opens the oyster, sucks the insides out,
　　Swallows it down… Our pilgrim pair,
　　Watching, aghast, stand gaping there,
Whereat Pierre, in quite the judgely tone,
Burbles: "Messieurs, the court's decision? Well…
For each of you, gratis, an oyster shell!"
　　So, please beware, all you too prone
To plead your cause. Today, not yours the gain.
The judge will keep the fees; and, for your pain,
　　You get the empty sack, no victuals;
　　No ball to bowl with, just the skittles.[2]

IX, 9

165

Le Loup et le Chien Maigre

Autrefois Carpillon fretin
Eut beau prêcher, il eut beau dire;
On le mit dans la poësle à frire.
Je fis voir que lâcher ce qu'on a dans la main,
Sous espoir de grosse avanture,
Est imprudence toute pure.
Le Pêcheur eut raison; Carpillon n'eut pas tort.
Chacun dit ce qu'il peut pour défendre sa vie.
Maintenant il faut que j'appuye
Ce que j'avançay lors de quelque trait encor.
Certain Loup, aussi sot que le pêcheur fut sage,
Trouvant un Chien hors du village,
S'en alloit l'emporter; le Chien representa
Sa maigreur: Ja ne plaise à vostre seigneurie
De me prendre en cet estat-là;
Attendez, mon maistre marie
Sa fille unique. Et vous jugez
Qu'estant de nopce, il faut mal-gré moy que j'engraisse.
Le Loup le croit, le Loup le laisse;
Le Loup quelques jours écoulez
Revient voir si son Chien n'est point meilleur à prendre.
Mais le drôle estoit au logis.
Il dit au Loup par un treillis:
Amy, je vais sortir. Et, si tu veux attendre,
Le portier du logis et moy
Nous serons tout à l'heure à toy.
Ce portier du logis estoit un Chien énorme,
Expediant les Loups en forme.
Celuy-cy s'en douta. Serviteur au portier,
Dit-il, et de courir. Il estoit fort agile;
Mais il n'estoit pas fort habile.
Ce Loup ne sçavoit pas encor bien son métier.

The Wolf and the Scrawny Dog

I told about a baby carp before—
    Fit to be fried, and little more—
Caught by a fisherman, ready to kill it
    And fling it, forthwith, in his skillet.[1]
My fable showed that it is folly pure
To scoff at fortune's offering until it
Offers us something better. No, for sure,
A carplet in the hand, I would opine,
Is worth two in the sea! That tale of mine
Proved it, though both the fish and fisherman
Acted as it behooved them: one, to dine;
And one, to save his skin and flee the pan!
    Now let me, with this tale, endeavor
    To add more proof… A wolf there was,
As stupid as that fisherman was clever:
    Catching a stray dog in his claws,
He bore the prize away. The dog, thereon,
Points out how small he is, how thin and wan:
    "Better Your Lordship wait, because
None will he be the worse for tarrying.
Shortly my master will be marrying
His only daughter off. No scrawny pup
Will I be then, but plump and fattened up!"
    The wolf believes him, and he leaves
Him there. A day or two go by, and then
Friend wolf returns, looks for his prey again.
    After a couple of *"qui vive?"*s
Friend dog, at home, snarls through the gate. Says he:
    "The warder and myself will be
Joining you shortly." Now, said warder
Happens to be a monstrous hound, the kind
    That sends wolves packing in short order!
Suspecting which, our wolf is ill-inclined
    To loll about! And, dull of mind
Though fleet of paw, he flees. Me, I'm afraid
He's one wolf who has yet to learn his trade!

Rien de Trop

Je ne vois point de creature
Se comporter modérement.
Il est certain temperament
Que le maistre de la nature
Veut que l'on garde en tout. Le fait-on? Nullement.
Soit en bien, soit en mal, cela n'arrive guere.
Le blé, riche present de la blonde Cerés
Trop touffu bien souvent épuise les guerets;
En superfluitez s'épandant d'ordinaire,
Et poussant trop abondamment,
Il oste à son fruit l'aliment.
L'arbre n'en fait pas moins; tant le luxe sçait plaire.
Pour corriger le blé, Dieu permit aux moutons
De retrancher l'excés des prodigues moissons.
Tout au travers ils se jetterent,
Gasterent tout, et tout brouterent,
Tant que le Ciel permit aux Loups
D'en croquer quelques-uns: ils les croquerent tous.
S'ils ne le firent pas, du moins ils y tâcherent.
Puis le Ciel permit aux humains
De punir ces derniers: les humains abuserent
A leur tour des ordres divins.
De tous les animaux l'homme a le plus de pente
A se porter dedans l'excés.
Il faudroit faire le procés
Aux petits comme aux grands. Il n'est ame vivante
Qui ne peche en cecy. Rien de trop, est un point
Dont on parle sans cesse, et qu'on n'observe point.

All in Moderation

Animal, Man, or vegetation:
No living thing on this our sphere
But fails to act in moderation,
Wisely, as Nature's overseer
Would have us do. But do we? Never!
Whether for bale or benefit, whichever!
To prove my point: fair Ceres' gift of grain [1]
Often will overspread the fallow plain
In such a lush excess that much will lie
    Unnourished and, in time, must die.
    (Trees too, delightful luxuries!)
    To save the wheat God let the sheep
Feed on its wealth of superfluities.
But they (the sheep) were ill inclined to keep
Their appetite in check: they gorged, they glutted,
    Such that, I think you'll find, they gutted
    All of the grain; whereat God let
The wolves feed on the sheep: "Go, eat a few…"
    They ate them all, as wolves will do—
Or tried, at least, with wolfly etiquette.
    To carry out the wolves' chastisement
    God turned to Man. But he (the latter),
    Prone only to his aggrandizement,
Spurning God's orders, promptly made the matter
Really no better, even worse. And all
Are guilty: humans great and humans small,
    Humans of every stripe and station.
    Listen to Man the Overweening:
    "Yes," he cries, "all in moderation,"
Only to prove he doesn't know the meaning.

IX, 11

Les Poissons et le Cormoran

Il n'estoit point d'étang dans tout le voisinage
Qu'un Cormoran n'eust mis à contribution.
Viviers et reservoirs luy payoient pension:
Sa cuisine alloit bien; mais lors que le long âge
  Eut glacé le pauvre animal,
  La mesme cuisine alla mal.
Tout Cormoran se sert de pourvoyeur luy-mesme.
Le nostre un peu trop vieux pour voir au fond des eaux,
  N'ayant ny filets ny rezeaus,
  Souffroit une disette extreme.
Que fit-il? Le besoin, docteur en stratagême,
Luy fournit celuy-ci. Sur le bord d'un Estang
  Cormoran vid une Ecrevisse.
Ma commere, dit-il, allez tout à l'instant
  Porter un avis important
  A ce peuple. Il faut qu'il perisse:
Le maistre de ce lieu dans huit jours peschera.
  L'Ecrevisse en haste s'en va
  Conter le cas: grande est l'émute.

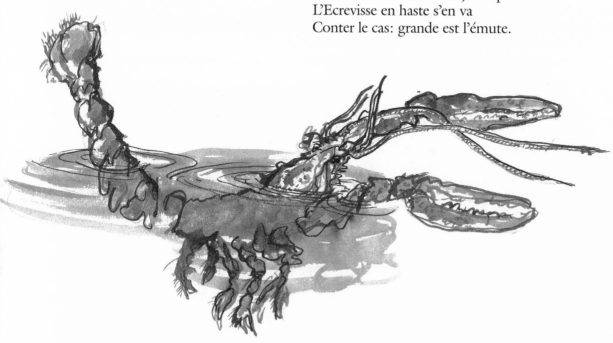

The Fishes and the Cormorant

No marsh was there, nearby or out beyond
　　For miles around, no pool, no pond,
Wherein a certain cormorant had not
　　Levied his due of fish! Full well,
Indeed, he dined upon that clientele
　　For many a pleasant year. But what
　　To do, alas, when, with the chill
Of age, that bill of fare treated him ill?
　　Now, cormorants fend for themselves.
But ours, clouded of eye, no longer delves
Deep in the waters, as when he was younger;
　　And, having neither net nor line,
　　Languishes, deeper yet, in hunger.
Necessity, that doctor of design
And ruse, found him a useful stratagem.
Spying a crayfish by a shore: "Ahem,
Ma sœur," he says, approaching. "Please, be good
Enough to warn those in the neighborhood
　　That I have woesome news for them.
Their end is near! For, I have heard it said,

On court, on s'assemble, on députe
A l'oiseau: Seigneur Cormoran,
D'où vous vient cet avis? quel est vostre garand?
Estes-vous seur de cette affaire?
N'y sçavez-vous remede? et qu'est-il bon de faire?
—Changer de lieu, dit il.—Comment le ferons-nous?
—N'en soyez point en soin: je vous porteray tous
L'un apres l'autre en ma retraite.
Nul que Dieu seul et moy n'en connoist les chemins,
Il n'est demeure plus secrete.
Un Vivier que nature y creusa de ses mains,
Inconnu des traitres humains,
Sauvera vostre republique.
On le crust. Le peuple aquatique
L'un apres l'autre fut porté
Sous ce rocher peu frequenté.
Là Cormoran le bon apostre,
Les ayant mis en un endroit
Transparent, peu creux, fort étroit,
Vous les prenoit sans peine, un jour l'un, un jour l'autre.
Il leur apprit à leurs dêpens
Que l'on de doit jamais avoir de confiance
En ceux qui sont mangeurs de gens.
Ils y perdirent peu, puis que l'humaine engeance
En auroit aussi bien croqué sa bonne part;
Qu'importe qui vous mange? homme ou loup; toute panse
Me paroist une à cet égard;
Un jour plustost, un jour plus tard,
Ce n'est pas grande difference.

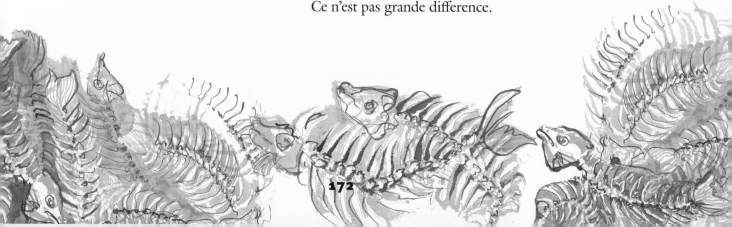

Next week the master of this pond intends
   To fish it clean! All of your friends,
   I hear, are soon to end up dead!"
The crayfish scuttles off to spread the word.
   Much the alarm and consternation
Among the fish; they send a delegation
   To put their questions to our bird.
"Seigneur, how do you know that what you heard
Is true?… And, if it is, what can we do?
Is there no help, no hope?… What? None?…" "Yes, one:
Flee to some other place, or be undone!"
"Some other place? But how?…" "I'll carry you,
One at a time, to my retreat, that none
   Can find but God above and me!
   A spring that, in her artistry,
Nature wrought with her hands, unknown to that
Cruel traitor they call Man! Secure will be
The nation Fish in its new habitat!"
Deceived, they all believe him. Day by day,
And one by one, off to his hideaway
He spirits them: a spot shallow and clear,
   Amidst the rocks, where, for his pleasure,
   Cormorant—hypocrite compeer—
   Consumes them at his whim and leisure.
Thus did he teach them—high the price, I fear!—
Not to trust those who eat their fellows! Still,
What difference, cormorant or man? The latter,
Sooner or later, would have gulped his fill!
Belly for belly: man's, bird's, wolf's… No matter.[1]

X, 3

L'Araignée et l'Hirondelle

O Jupiter, qui sceus de ton cerveau,
Par un secret d'acouchement nouveau,
Tirer Pallas, jadis mon ennemie,
Entends ma plainte une fois en ta vie.
Progné me vient enlever les morceaus;
Caracolant, frisant l'air et les eaus,
Elle me prend mes mouches à ma porte:
Miennes je puis les dire; et mon rezeau
En seroit plein sans ce maudit oyseau:
Je l'ay tissu de matiere assez forte.
    Ainsi, d'un discours insolent,
Se plaignoit l'Araignée autrefois tapissiere,
    Et qui lors estant filandiere
Pretendoit enlacer tout insecte volant.
La sœur de Philomele, attentive à sa proye,
Malgré le bestion happoit mouches dans l'air,
Pour ses petits, pour elle, impitoyable joye,
Que ses enfans gloutons, d'un bec toûjours ouvert,
D'un ton demy formé, bégayante couvée,
Demandoient par des cris encor mal entendus.
    La pauvre Aragne, n'ayant plus
Que la teste et les pieds, artisans superflus,
    Se vid elle-mesme enlevée.
L'hirondelle en passant emporta toile, et tout,
    Et l'animal pendant au bout.

Jupin pour chaque état mit deux tables au monde.
L'adroit, le vigilant, et le fort sont assis
    A la premiere; et les petits
    Mangent leur reste à la seconde.

The Spider and the Swallow

"O Jupiter, I pray you hear my plea,
    Once in your life! You who, somehow,
With some new, secret childbirth mystery,
Knew how to spawn my mortal enemy,
    Pallas, a-borning from your brow! [1]
    Procne, I'll have you know—a-flit,
    A-flutter, grazing sea and skies—
    Flies up before my wondering eyes,
    Comes to my house and, plundering it
(Damned bird!), makes off with all my horde of flies!
Mine, do you hear? My own! Why, but for her,
    My web would be chock full! I spun it
Of strongest thread—not some mere gossamer!—
So tough that it holds fast each mother's son it
    Lures to its grasping snare!…" So went
    The spider's rather insolent
Harangue: she, weaver *extraordinaire*
Of erstwhile artful tapestries; now spinner
    Of webs wherein to catch her dinner.
"The swallow," she complains, "is always there
To seize, upon the wing, my insect fare,
Both for herself and for her sputtering brood,
    Filling, with much solicitude,
Their gaping beaks!…" At length—now but a head
And feet that have no further use, in fact—
    She sees her web, straightway ransacked,
    As mother swallow, wings outspread,
    Carries the whole thing off, intact,
Trailing poor spider, dangling from a thread.

Jove sets two tables for each living kind.
The strong, the clever, and the quick of mind
    Sit at the first; the small, bereft,
Sit at the second, glad to get what's left.

X, 6

Les Poissons et le Berger
Qui Joue de la Flûte

Tyrcis qui pour la seule Annette
Faisoit resonner les accords
D'une voix et d'une musette
Capables de toucher les morts,
Chantoit un jour le long des bords
D'une onde arrosant des prairies,
Dont Zephire habitoit les campagnes fleuries.
Annette cependant à la ligne peschoit;
Mais nul poisson ne s'approchoit.
La Bergere perdoit ses peines.
Le Berger qui par ses chansons
Eust attiré des inhumaines,
Crut, et crut mal, attirer des poissons.
Il leur chanta cecy: Citoyens de cette onde,
Laissez vostre Nayade en sa grote profonde.
Venez voir un objet mille fois plus charmant.
Ne craignez point d'entrer aux prisons de la Belle:
Ce n'est qu'à nous qu'elle est cruelle:
Vous serez traitez doucement,
On n'en veut point à vostre vie:
Un vivier vous attend plus clair que fin cristal.
Et quand à quelques-uns l'appast seroit fatal,
Mourir des mains d'Annette est un sort que j'envie.
Ce discours éloquent ne fit pas grand effet:

The Fishes and the Shepherd
Who Plays the Flute

Tircis, a shepherd troubadour[1]—
Who sang and droned his bagpipe for
The fair Annette—whose rustic song
Could charm the dead, one day, along
A meadow-stream's lush-flowering shore,
Zephyr-caressed, was singing; whilst Annette
Sat angling by the rivulet.
The shepherdess, however, had
No luck whatever; not one fish drew near
Her dangling line. Wherefore our lad,
Ever the gallant country cavalier,
Sure to bring round the hardest heart
With his boundless, melodious art,
Assumes—amiss!—that he need merely sing
To summon fish. He does. And this is what
He sings: "Denizens of this spring,
Come, leave your nymph, your naiad! Linger not
Amid her grotto deeps. Come gaze upon
An object rare, a true phenomenon
Of beauteousness, a thousand times more fair!
Fear not! Her Loveliness has no intent
Here to entrap you in her snare.
Alas, her cruelty is meant
For none but me. For you, she will prepare
A crystal pond where, fancy-free,
You will be served[2] with much gentility
And grace. And even if, perhaps,
One or a few of you might, by some lapse,

177

L'auditoire estoit sourd aussi bien que muet.
Tyrcis eut beau prescher: ses paroles miellées
    S'en estant aux vents envolées,
Il tendit un long rets. Voila les poissons pris,
Voila les poissons mis aux pieds de la Bergere.
O vous Pasteurs d'humains et non pas de brebis,
Rois qui croyez gagner par raisons les esprits
    D'une multitude étrangere,
Ce n'est jamais par-là que l'on en vient à bout;
    Il y faut une autre maniere:
Servez-vous de vos rets, la puissance fait tout.

Bite of the deadly hook, and be
Undone, ah me! my fish coquettes,
How I myself would envy such a fate:
To die at hands as gracious as Annette's!"
Blown to the winds, his honeyed words! The bait
Lures not one fish. Therewith does Tircis cast
A net… Wait… Pull it in, replete,
As full as full can be! And there, amassed
Before the shepherdess's feet,
Fishes galore!… O kings, you shepherds who
Gather up humans in your retinue,
Woo not Man's mind with vain conceit!
Power is all: spread wide your nets. For then,
Like fish, so also shall it be with men.

X, 10

179

Le Songe d'un Habitant du Mogol

Jadis certain Mogol vid en songe un Vizir,
Aux champs Eliziens possesseur d'un plaisir
Aussi pur qu'infini, tant en prix qu'en durée;
Le mesme songeur vid en une autre contrée
  Un Hermite entouré de feux,
Qui touchoit de pitié mesme les mal-heureux.
Le cas parut étrange, et contre l'ordinaire;
Minos en ces deux morts sembloit s'estre mépris.
Le dormeur s'éveilla, tant il en fut surpris.
Dans ce songe pourtant soupçonnant du mystere,
  Il se fit expliquer l'affaire.

The Dream of the Man from Mogol Land

A certain Mogol had a dream. In it
He saw, in the Elysian Fields,[1] a rich
Vizier blessed with a joy—pure, infinite;
   Then saw another land in which
   A godly hermit stood, surrounded,
Verily, by hell's fire, in such cruel wise
That even those by misery confounded
Gazed with much sad compassion in their eyes.
The dream astounded him; was quite contrary
   To what one might deem right! Had Minos,
   Possibly—His Infernal Highness!—
Erred in his retributions customary?
   In awe, the dreamer woke. "There ought

L'interprete luy dit: Ne vous étonnez point,
Vostre songe a du sens, et si j'ay sur ce poinct
      Acquis tant soit peu d'habitude,
C'est un avis des Dieux. Pendant l'humain séjour,
Ce Vizir quelquesfois cherchoit la solitude;
Cét Hermite aux Vizirs alloit faire sa cour.

Si j'osois ajoûter au mot de l'interprete,
J'inspirerois icy l'amour de la retraite:
Elle offre à ses amans des biens sans embarras,
Biens purs, presens du Ciel, qui naissent sous les pas.
Solitude où je trouve une douceur secrete,
Lieux que j'aimay toûjours, ne pourray-je jamais,
Loin du monde et du bruit goûter l'ombre et le frais?
O qui m'arrestera sous vos sombres aziles!
Quand pourront les neuf Sœurs, loin des cours et des Villes
M'occuper tout entier, et m'apprendre des Cieux
Les divers mouvemens inconnus à nos yeux,
Les noms et les vertus de ces clartez errantes,
Par qui sont nos destins et nos mœurs differentes?
Que si je ne suis né pour de si grands projets,
Du moins que les ruisseaux m'offrent de doux objets!
Que je peigne en mes Vers quelque rive fleurie!
La Parque à filets d'or n'ourdira point ma vie;
Je ne dormiray point sous de riches lambris;
Mais void-on que le somme en perde de son prix?
En est-il moins profond, et moins plein de délices?
Je luy vouë au desert de nouveaux sacrifices.
Quand le moment viendra d'aller trouver les morts,
J'auray vescu sans soins, et mourray sans remords.

Be some good explanation," so he thought.
    A soothsayer told him: "Friend, I read
The truth behind your dream; forsooth, you need
No further seek. It shows the gods' opinion:
In life your rich vizier—that courtly minion—
Sought solitude; whilst your ascetic sort
Yearned in his heart to toady at the Court."

Should I dare add a word, I would but try
To sing, in gentle and bucolic mood,
The treasures unalloyed that solitude
Offers to those who love it, as do I;
Gifts heaven-sent, in rich abundance: pure
Solace of unspoiled pleasure, quiet retreat,
Refuge from city's bustle! When will your
Cool leisure-shades let me partake your sweet
Repose, far from the world of town, of men,
Of court? Perhaps the Muses—sisters nine—
Will come and lodge within my bosom then,
And let me learn the heavens' dark, mute design—
Taciturn, but writ on the stars!—whereby
Our destinies, unknowing, intertwine! [2]
Or, if too grandiose that scheme, then I
Will dwell at least by stream and brook, and fill
My book with flowering banks! So? Clotho will
Not weave my life with threads of gold brocade; [3]
Nor shall I lie midst ceilings, walls, inlaid
With wealth. But will my slumber be less deep?
Less calm my rest? Less pleasure-blessed my sleep?
Nay. I will keep my vow, to nature made:
Care-free, my life; and, with my final breath,
Free of remorse as well when I face death.

XI, 4

183

Le Loup et le Renard

Mais d'où vient qu'au Renard Esope accorde un poinct?
C'est d'exceller en tours pleins de matoiserie.
J'en cherche la raison, et ne la trouve point.
Quand le Loup a besoin de défendre sa vie,
    Ou d'attaquer celle d'autruy,
    N'en sçait-il pas autant que luy?
Je crois qu'il en sçait plus, et j'oserois peut-estre
Avec quelque raison contredire mon maistre.
Voicy pourtant un cas où tout l'honneur échût
A l'hoste des terriers. Un soir il apperçeut
La Lune au fond d'un puits: l'orbiculaire image
    Luy parut un ample fromage.
    Deux sceaux alternativement
    Puisoient le liquide élement.
Nostre Renard pressé par une faim canine,
S'accommode en celuy qu'au haut de la machine

184

The Wolf and the Fox

Why, when it comes to artifice and wile,
   Does Æsop, that great fable bard,
My master, hold the fox in such regard?
   Is not the wolf as full of guile
   When faced with peril, or when he
Plies his attack against an enemy?
   Fuller, in fact! I think I could
Argue the matter, in all likelihood,
If I so chose. But, for the moment, I
Shall tell a tale with which to justify
That high regard for Sire Renard… One night,
As, in the moonlight, he was passing by
A well, he looked and saw, down deep, the bright,
   Round fullness of the moon's reflection,

L'autre sceau tenoit suspendu.

Voilà l'animal descendu,

Tiré d'erreur, mais fort en peine,

Et voyant sa perte prochaine.

Car comment remonter si quelque autre affamé

De la mesme image charmé,

Et succedant à sa misere,

Par le mesme chemin ne le tiroit d'affaire?

Deux jours s'estoient passez sans qu'aucun vinst au puits;

Le temps qui toûjours marche avoit pendant deux nuits

Echancré selon l'ordinaire

De l'astre au front d'argent la face circulaire.

Sire Renard estoit desesperé.

Compere Loup, le gosier alteré,

Passe par là; l'autre dit: Camarade,

Je vous veux régaler; voyez-vous cét objet?

C'est un fromage exquis. Le Dieu Faune l'a fait,

La vache Io donna le laict.

Jupiter, s'il estoit malade,

Reprendroit l'appetit en tastant d'un tel mets.

J'en ay mangé cette échancrure,

Le reste vous sera suffisante pasture.

Descendez dans un sceau que j'ay là mis exprés.

Bien qu'au moins mal qu'il pust il ajustast l'histoire,

Le Loup fut un sot de le croire.

Il descend, et son poids, emportant l'autre part,

Reguinde en haut maistre Renard.

Ne nous en mocquons point: nous nous laissons séduire

Sur aussi peu de fondement;

Et chacun croit fort aisément

Ce qu'il craint, et ce qu'il desire.

And thought the orb, upon inspection,
To be a cheese. With bucket after bucket
    (For two there were) he tried to drain
Said well, hoping thereby, in time, to pluck it.
No luck… Famished, he takes the buckets twain,
Sits in the one suspended high, descends—
    Soon disabused, dismayed!—and spends
Many an anxious moment, chastened now,
    And wondering what to do! For, how
To rise, unless another hungry one,
Fooled too, decides to do what he has done!…
Two days go by, and no one comes… Two nights
As well, taking Time's customary bites
Out of the silver-browed celestial sphere.
    Renard grows desperate. Then, at last,
    The wolf, a-thirst, comes ambling past.
"Compère," cries fox, "see what I have down here:
This luscious cheese that Pan himself has pressed
    From Io's very milk! [1] Why, were
Jupiter out of sorts, this dish would stir
His appetite, I vow! I've saved the rest
For you! Now, see that bucket? Come, get in it.
    I put it there with you in mind."
    The wolf, too readily inclined
To be undone, complies. In but a minute
Down does he come; up goes the fox; no doubt
Leaving the wolf to ponder his way out.
    But let's not mock him: Man, no less,
    Is easily led by the ear;
Only too willing, we, to acquiesce
To what we wish—or even dread!—to hear.

XI, 6

Les Souris et le Chat-huant

Il ne faut jamais dire aux gens:
Ecoûtez un bon mot, oyez une merveille.
Sçavez-vous si les écoûtans
En feront une estime à la vostre pareille?
Voicy pourtant un cas qui peut estre excepté.
Je le maintiens prodige, et tel que d'une Fable
Il a l'air et les traits, encor que veritable.
On abattit un pin pour son antiquité,
Vieux Palais d'un hibou, triste et sombre retraite
De l'oiseau qu'Atropos prend pour son interprete.
Dans son tronc caverneux, et miné par le temps,
Logeoient entre autres habitans
Force souris sans pieds, toutes rondes de graisse.
L'oyseau les nourrissoit parmy des tas de bled,
Et de son bec avoit leur troupeau mutilé;
Cét Oyseau raisonnoit, il faut qu'on le confesse.
En son temps aux Souris le compagnon chassa.
Les premieres qu'il prit du logis échapées,
Pour y remedier, le drôle estropia
Tout ce qu'il prit en suite. Et leurs jambes coupées
Firent qu'il les mangeoit à sa commodité,
Aujourd'huy l'une, et demain l'autre.
Tout manger à la fois, l'impossibilité
S'y trouvoit, joint aussi le soin de sa santé.
Sa prévoyance alloit aussi loin que la nostre;
Elle alloit jusqu'à leur porter
Vivres et grains pour subsister.
Puis, qu'un Cartesien s'obstine
A traiter ce hibou de montre et de machine!
Quel ressort luy pouvoit donner
Le conseil de tronquer un peuple mis en muë?
Si ce n'est pas là raisonner,
La raison m'est chose inconnuë.

The Mice and the Screech Owl

Never tell someone: "Friend, you'll never
Believe the tale I'm going to tell!" Whatever
Wonders you would regale him with, the fact
Remains that someone else may not react
    With as much awe as you. However,
Let me here make exception. For, what now
I am about to tell you will, I vow,
Seem like a miracle. What's more, although
It might appear to be a fiction, it's
    The utter truth. Not long ago
    A tree was being hacked to bits;
A pine, old and decayed, whose time-worn bark
Concealed a screech owl's lodging: dismal, dark
Refuge of Atropos's favorite creature. [1]
Its hollow trunk, beside said somber screecher,
Played host to other beasts as well: a horde
    Of mice especially—round, fat,
    And… footless! Quite so! There they sat,
    Amid the food the owl kept stored
    To fatten up his captives! Yes,
It was the bird who, chewing off their paws,
    Held them there, plump and powerless!
That owl could reason, to be sure. Because
    The mice he'd caught before, and brought
To his abode, would all escape, he thought:
"Best I unpaw them, keep them here, and mete
Them out, at meals, each day, at will. To eat
Them all at once would be unhealthy, and
Impossible to boot!" One must construe
The faculty of thinking here: he planned,
    Clearly, no less than we might do,
Amassing grains and such to feed his prey.
    So, let Cartesians have their say;
A mere machine, this creature? [2] No. If you
Can see no reason here, I know not what

Voyez que d'argumens il fit:
      Quand ce peuple est pris, il s'enfuit:
Donc il faut le croquer aussi-tost qu'on le hape.
Tout: il est impossible. Et puis pour le besoin
N'en dois-je pas garder? Donc il faut avoir soin
      De le nourrir sans qu'il échape.
Mais comment? Ostons-luy les pieds. Or trouvez-moy
Chose par les humains à sa fin mieux conduite.
Quel autre art de penser Aristote et sa suite
      Enseignent-ils par vostre foy?

Cecy n'est point une Fable, et la chose quoyque merveilleuse et presque incroyable, est véritablement arrivée. J'ay peut estre porté trop loin la prévoyance de ce hibou; car je ne pretends pas établir dans les bestes un progrés de raisonnement tel que celuy-cy; mais ces exagerations sont permises à la Poësie, sur tout dans la maniere d'écrire dont je me sers.

To call it then! I pray you look
At all the subtle steps it took:
  "These folk flee when I catch them; but,
Though I would eat them, one and all, it's not
Easy to gulp so many on the spot!
Besides, it's best to keep a few for later;
Which means I'll have to feed them, and take care
Lest they go trotting off." So, then and there,
  Concludes our ratiocinator:
"How? Well, by biting off their paws!" No doubt,
Worthy of Aristotle, this: thought out
With art surpassing Man the Meditator!

*This is not a fiction; the event, though wondrous and almost
unbelievable, did, indeed, take place. Perhaps I have pushed
this owl's foresight a bit too far; I do not claim animals to
have as well-developed a capacity to reason as did this one; but
such exaggerations are permitted in poetry, especially in the
style of which I make use in mine.* 3

XI, 9

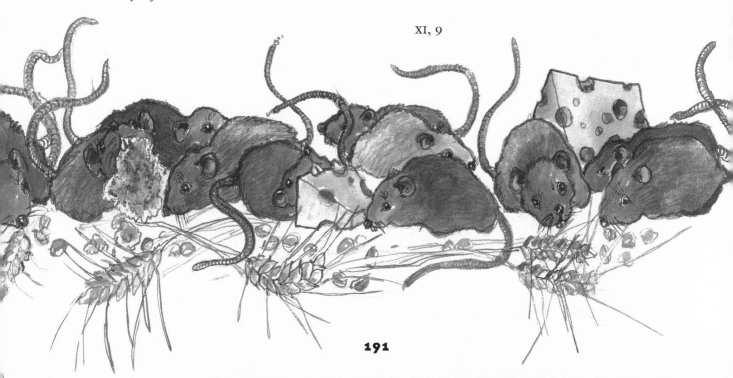

Du Thésauriseur et du Singe

Un Homme accumuloit. On sçait que cette erreur
  Va souvent jusqu'à la fureur.
Celui-ci ne songeoit que Ducats et Pistoles.
Quand ces biens sont oisifs, je tiens qu'ils sont frivoles.
  Pour seureté de son Tresor,
Nôtre Avare habitoit un lieu dont Amphitrite
Défendoit aux voleurs de toutes parts l'abord.
Là d'une volupté selon moy fort petite,
Et selon lui fort grande, il entassoit toûjours.
  Il passoit les nuits et les jours
A compter, calculer, supputer sans relâche,
Calculant, supputant, comptant, comme à la tâche,
Car il trouvoit toûjours du mécompte à son fait:
Un gros Singe plus sage, à mon sens, que son maître,
Jettoit quelque Doublon toûjours par la fenêtre,
  Et rendoit le compte imparfait.
  La chambre bien cadenacée
Permettoit de laisser l'argent sur le comptoir.
Un beau jour Dom-bertrand se mit dans la pensée
D'en faire un sacrifice au liquide manoir.
  Quant à moi, lors que je compare
Les plaisirs de ce Singe à ceux de cet Avare,
Je ne sçai bonnement ausquels donner le prix.
Dom-bertrand gagneroit prés de certains esprits;
Les raisons en seroient trop longues à déduire.
Un jour donc l'animal, qui ne songeoit qu'à nuire,
Détachoit du monceau tantôt quelque Doublon,
  Un Jacobus, un Ducaton,
  Et puis quelque Noble à la rose;
Éprouvoit son adresse et sa force à jetter
Ces morceaux de métail qui se font souhaiter

The Treasure-Hoarder and the Ape

A miser once there was who stored and stored
His wealth. We know, I think, to what extent
    Such avaricious temperament
Can lead to folly: gold and silver hoard,
Unspent, and left to rot in idleness,
    Serves little use. But I digress…
    To keep his treasure safe, Monsieur
Lived in a house surrounded by the sea
    (Protected on all sides by her
Whom god Poseidon called his spouse). And he
Would gloat, day in day out, nighttime no less,
    Lusting—although I find the word
A bit too strong, and him a bit absurd!—
    With fondest, tenderest caress,
Counting his ducats, weighing them, and then
Counting them yet once more, and yet again;
For always did he find his count amiss,
    The reason for which being this:
An ape—wiser, perhaps, than he, indeed!—
Dwelt by his side. Since tightly lock-and-keyed
His quarters, all our miser's wealth could lie
Unhidden, spread before the naked eye.
    Now, Dom Bertrand,[1] of prankish breed,
Daily, would throw a coin or two away
    Flinging them out the open window,
    Till, for some reason, one fine day,
Suddenly—Who knows why? Not I!—he grinned (Oh,
Truly a nasty grin!), made up his mind
To throw each blessèd sou into the sea!
No less a pleasant sport, if you ask me,
Than keeping it—though, if I were inclined
    To tell you why, you well might find

Par les humains sur toute chose.
S'il n'avoit entendu son Compteur à la fin
    Mettre la clef dans la serrure,
Les Ducats auroient tous pris le même chemin
    Et couru la même avanture.
Il les auroit fait tous voler, jusqu'au dernier,
Dans le goufre enrichi par maint et maint naufrage.
Dieu veüille préserver maint et maint Financier
    Qui n'en fait pas meilleur usage.

The explanation rather tedious.
Well, so it goes. One day, our mischievous
Monkey, alone, seizing them, one by one—
    Each metal disk Man covets so—
Hurled them with strength and skill. He would have done,
    Thus, the whole precious lot, but lo!
Before ducat, doubloon, and all the rest
Could fly, he hears Monsieur's key in the door!
Ah sea, by many a shipwreck treasure blessed,
How close you came to being enriched still more!
    I pray God grant long life and health
To financiers who, likewise, waste their wealth!

XII, 3

195

L'Aigle et la Pie

L'aigle Reine des airs, avec Margot la Pie,
Differentes d'humeur, de langage et d'esprit,
                    Et d'habit,
            Traversoient un bout de prairie.
Le hazard les assemble en un coin détourné.
L'Agasse eut peur; mais l'Aigle, aïant fort bien dîné,
La rassure, et luy dit: Allons de compagnie.
Si le Maître des Dieux assez souvent s'ennuie,
            Luy qui gouverne l'Univers,
J'en puis bien faire autant, moy qu'on sçait qui le sers.
Entretenez-moi donc, et sans ceremonie.
Caquet bon-bec alors de jaser au plus drû
Sur cecy, sur cela, sur tout. L'homme d'Horace
Disant le bien, le mal, à travers champ, n'eût sçû
Ce qu'en fait de babil y sçavoit nôtre Agasse.
Elle offre d'avertir de tout ce qui se passe,
            Sautant, allant de place en place,
Bon espion, Dieu sçait. Son offre aïant déplu,
            L'Aigle lui dit tout en colere:
            Ne quittez point vôtre sejour,
Caquet bon-bec, ma mie; adieu. Je n'ay que faire
            D'une babillarde à ma Cour:
            C'est un fort méchant caractere.
            Margot ne demandoit pas mieux.
Ce n'est pas ce qu'on croit, que d'entrer chez les Dieux,
Cet honneur a souvent de mortelles angoisses.
Rediseurs, Espions, gens à l'air gracieux,
Au cœur tout different, s'y rendent odieux,
Quoi qu'ainsi que la Pie il faille dans ces lieux
            Porter habit de deux parroisses.

The Eagle and the Magpie

One day the eagle, sovereign of the sky,
Queen of the spacious realm, and Mag the pie—
Different in nature, humor, tongue, no less
      Than dress—
  Were flying by a field, when each,
  As luck would have it, chanced to reach
The selfsame spot. The pie, as you might guess,
Was struck with terror. But the eagle had
  Already supped her fill, and bade
Her have no fear. "Let's you and me," she says,
"Travel in one another's company.
I think you could be good for my malaise:
If Jove himself knows moments of ennui,
Why shouldn't I, who serve His Majesty!
So, entertain me with your chatter." Ha!
  No sooner thus invited than
Dame Blabbermouth begins her bla-bla-bla,
On this, on that, on everything. That man
  We read about, of Horace's,
Could not sing so much gossip—bad or good
(Solos, recitatives, and choruses!)[1]—
As does our Mag! At length she says she would
Make a fine spy: fly here, fly there, report
All that she saw… Queen Eagle, quick to scoff her,
  Angry, rejects the prattler's offer.
  "Back whence you came, my friend! My court
  Needs no vile tattlers of your sort!"
  Mag, happy to escape, flies off, her
Lesson now learned. To wit: there's not much glory
Serving the great. (Kings… Gods, *a fortiori!*)
Spies, tattletales, for all the charms they proffer—
And, like the pie, sporting her colors double[2]—
  Cause nothing with their pains but trouble.

XII, II

197

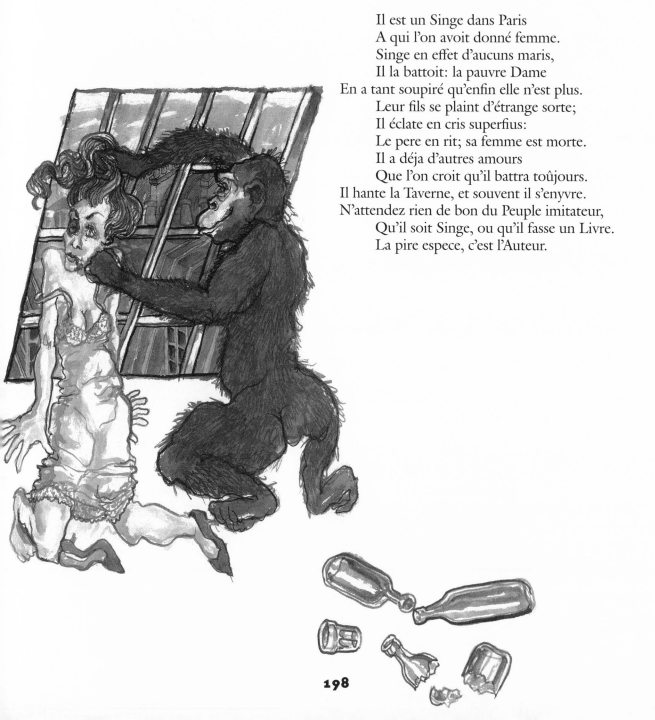

Le Singe

Il est un Singe dans Paris
A qui l'on avoit donné femme.
Singe en effet d'aucuns maris,
Il la battoit: la pauvre Dame
En a tant soupiré qu'enfin elle n'est plus.
Leur fils se plaint d'étrange sorte;
Il éclate en cris superfius:
Le pere en rit; sa femme est morte.
Il a déja d'autres amours
Que l'on croit qu'il battra toûjours.
Il hante la Taverne, et souvent il s'enyvre.
N'attendez rien de bon du Peuple imitateur,
Qu'il soit Singe, ou qu'il fasse un Livre.
La pire espece, c'est l'Auteur.

The Ape

A certain ape, in Paris, took a wife—
A human one—and aped those husbands who
   Batter their helpless mates. He too
Beat her within a hairsbreadth of her life,
    Until, with many sobs and sighs,
       The lady dies.
Their son laments, cries, raises quite a stir.
No use! The father laughs: that wife is dead.
   Now other loves has he to bed,
Ones that, no doubt, he'll beat as much as her.
Drunkard, he haunts the tavern, slakes his thirst…
Expect no virtue from these would-be men:
   Whether with grimace or with pen,
Vile imitators! But the most accursed—
The author-ape!—dear reader, is the worst! [1]

XII, 19

Notes

Death and the Wretched Man, & Death and the Woodsman

1. Mæcenas, whose reflection La Fontaine cites below, and whom he praises in the prose passage following the fable, was an important Roman patron of letters during the reign of Augustus. Henri Regnier, in his *Œuvres de J. de la Fontaine* (rev. ed., 11 vols. [Paris: Hachette, 1883–92], 1, 103–06), indicates that La Fontaine probably knew his lines of verse either as quoted in one of Seneca's *Epistles* or as referred to by Montaigne in his *Essays* (11, 37).

2. The *corvée* referred to in the original was the labor imposed upon private citizens in the service of the king or lord. The practice was not abolished until the revolution of 1789.

The Hornets and the Honeybees

1. Announcing his moral, as he sometimes does, at the beginning rather than the end of his fable, La Fontaine cites a line from Aristophanes' comedy *The Thesmophiriazusæ* ("The Women at Demeter's Feast"), of 411 B.C., more commonly quoted as "A l'œuvre on connaît l'ouvrier."

2. I have avoided a literal translation, which would be lost in English, of the French *lécher l'ours* ("to lick the bear"), a literary allusion borrowed from Rabelais (*Pantagruel*, Book III, chapter 42) and applied to unnecessarily long and drawn-out proceedings, legal and otherwise.

3. In La Fontaine's time the arbitrariness, severity, and venality of Turkish justice were a literary commonplace based largely on fact. (See Regnier, *Op. cit.*, 1, 122.)

4. For a later fable that dramatizes this observation, see "The Oyster and the Adversaries" (pp. 164–65).

The Rats in Council Assembled

1. La Fontaine borrows the name of the cat, Rodilard(us), from Rabelais (*Pantagruel*, Book IV, chapter 67).

2.   The question forms the recurring line in the 14th-century fabulist Eustache Deschamps's treatment of the same fable in *ballade* form. (See my collection *The Fabulists French: Verse Fables of Nine Centuries* [Urbana: University of Illinois Press, 1992], pp. 10–11).

3.   For a list of some of the dozens of Oriental and Occidental antecedents and adaptations of this popular tale, probably introduced to the West by the Arabs in the 13th century, see Paul Franklin Baum, "The Fable of Belling the Cat," in *Proverbia in Fabula: Essays on the Relationship of the Proverb and the Fable*, ed. Pack Carnes (Bern: Lang, 1988), pp. 37–46.

The Ass with a Load of Sponges and The Ass with a Load of Salt
1.   La Fontaine is no doubt referring here to the celebrated episode in Rabelais (*Pantagruel*, Book IV, chapter 8), in which Panurge loses all his sheep once he has lost the first.

The Hare and the Frogs
1.   As occasionally happens, owing to La Fontaine's somewhat capricious punctuation, it is not clear if the moral here is spoken by the hare or by the poet. I opt for the former.

The Drunkard and His Wife
1.   Regnier points out that, despite analogues as far back as Æsop, this tale—really a *conte* rather than a fable—was thought by some to be inspired be a true anecdote occurring between a lawyer and his wife in the year 1550. (See *Op. cit.*, 1, 223.)

2.   La Fontaine's choice of Alecto rather than either of her sister-Furies of Greco-Roman mythology, besides probably being dictated by exigencies of rhyme, was appropriate in that she, unlike Tisiphone (the avenger) and Megæra (the disputatious), was the implacable member of the trio.

3.   There is certainly a touch of irony intended here in La Fontaine's use of the noun *cellerière* in an infernal setting. Like its masculine equivalent, referring to the monk in charge of a monastery's edibles, the word, long archaic, was always used in a specifically ecclesiastical context.

Philomela and Procne
1.   The reader familiar with Ovid's *Metamorphoses* (Book VI, 412–676) will recall the tale of the two sisters, Procne (or Progne) and Philomela, turned into swallow and nightingale respectively, as a result of a nasty family squabble with the mythical King Tereus of Thrace. When the king, married to Procne, seduced her sister, he cut out

her tongue to keep her from telling; but Philomela cleverly revealed the news by stitching it into her embroidery. To avenge Tereus's infidelity, Procne killed his son and served him up for supper. His resulting rage would have led to the two sisters' deaths were it not for the gods, who took pity on them, and turned them into birds.

The Drowned Wife

1.   Without copying La Fontaine's quadruple rhyme in these concluding lines—a rare phenomenon in his work—I attempt to achieve something of the same effect, perhaps more subtly, with repetition, alliteration, and inner rhymes.

The Shepherd and the Sea

1.   The reader will appreciate La Fontaine's intention in contrasting the names Tircis and Corydon, on the one hand, with Pierrot, on the other. The former, from many a classical eclogue and Renaissance pastoral romance, bespeak a much more stylized and elegant simplicity than the latter, the very essence of earthiness and banality.

The Fly and the Ant

1.   This allusion, a translator's nightmare, refers, as La Fontaine's fly rightly informs us, to that cosmetic meaning of the noun *mouche*. Equally challenging is his punning reference, in line 40 of the original, to the noun *mouchard* ("squealer").

2.   This ant of La Fontaine's, staunch defender of the work ethic, is obviously a close, but much more loquacious, relative of the famous heroine of his first fable, "The Cricket and the Ant" (I, 1). (For my translation of same, see *Fifty Fables of La Fontaine* [Urbana: University of Illinois Press, 1988], pp. 2–3.)

ILLUST. The engraving *La Toilette* or *Peinture sans Maîtrise* by Nicolas Guérard (a contemporary of La Fontaine) is an obvious source for the lady applying her fly. D.S.

The Gardener and His Lord

1.   One can suppose a thinly-veiled off-color suggestion on the part of the *seigneur*, the *escarcelle* being, at the time, a little sack usually hung from the belt. (The reader should keep in mind that the analogous French noun *la bourse* ["purse"], in the plural, has also long been used to designate the scrotum.) Such—and more pointed—liberties are the stuff of which many of La Fontaine's *Contes et nouvelles en vers* are made. (See my volume *La Fontaine's Bawdy: Of Libertines, Louts, and Lechers* [Princeton: Princeton University Press, 1992], *passim*.)

2.   If I wanted to justify my onomastic liberty and the arithmetical exaggeration it entails, I could point out that, for the Romans, a large portion of southern France was, indeed, known as *Provincia*.

The War Between the Rats and the Weasels

1. Assuming a translator's license to indulge in name-play no less than La Fontaine, I choose here the obviously medieval-sounding "Rat le Bel"—a reference to the 13th-century king Philippe le Bel—and, below (line 25), "the Ratovingian host," to render, respectively, his *Ratapon* and *le peuple Souriquois*, the latter a conflation of *souris* ("mouse") and the then celebrated Iroquois.

2. Meridarpax ("bit-thief") and Psicarpax—or, more properly, Psicharpax ("crumb-thief")—are characters in the 303-line Greek mock-epic *Batrachomyomachia* ("The Battle of the Frogs and the Mice"), long attributed to Homer but most likely dating, anonymously, from the 6th century. No character named Artarpax ("bread-thief") actually appears in the text, though others with similarly compounded names do. (See Regnier, *Op. cit.*, I, 287.)

ILLUST. This text suggested so many varying periods of military history that I decided to picture the rats as Roman legions (with as much debt to Cecil B. de Mille as to Trajan's column), while for the Weasles I turned to Kathë Köllwitz's masterful etching "The March of the Weavers," 1907. D.S.

The Master's Eye

1. Since some of my readers may be a little less familiar with classical mythology than La Fontaine's, I add to his mention of the Roman goddess of agriculture, provider of grain, the appropriate adjective "fair," often associated with her.

2. The citation echoes the characteristically pithy moral of Phædrus's fable *Cervus et Boves* ("The Stag and the Oxen") (II, 8): *Haec significat fabula / Dominum videre plurimum in rebus suis* ("This fable means / That a master sees to his own affairs best").

The Lark, Her Little Ones, and the Farmer Who Owns the Field

1. This typical intrusion of a short line accentuates, in La Fontaine's original, his device—unusual but occasionally met with—of using a single rhyme over three lines. The present collection offers a number of examples.

ILLUST. Anyone familiar with French painting will immediately recognize these figures, based closely on the farmworkers of Jean-François Millet, or from Vincent Van Gogh's famous series "Moissonneurs à la faucille," painted not directly from the Millet canvases but from a series of etchings, after Millet, by Jacques Adrien Lavielle. The sower (p. 3) watched by "The Swallow and the Little Birds" also has his roots in these great works. D.S.

The Hare and His Ears

1.   For details regarding the mental hospital known as Les Petites-Maisons, founded in Paris in 1497, and whose name eventually came to be used generically, see Regnier, *Op. cit.*, I, 377.

ILLUST: When I saw the list of fables to be illustrated in this volume I worried about the lack of variety of animals. So many dogs, apes, wolves, asses, and lions, nothing very exotic; but an illustrator has no choice—I was grateful for the cormorant! Then I started thinking about this fable. The trophies in the Lion's den represent the horns of the Argali, the Zebu, the Markhor, the Klipspringer, the Gemsbok, the Pronghorn, the Nyala, the Saiga, the Sitatunga, the Whipiti, and the Yak (all of which sounds more like a list from Dr. Seuss than La Fontaine). I might add that the nodules on the yak horns are not natural but are made of brass or bell metal and are a decorative addition, hardly surprising considering that yaks also, as I observed on my recent sojourn in Sikhim, wear earrings. D.S.

The Old Woman and the Two Servants

1.   A thoroughgoing classicist, La Fontaine is, of course, alluding to the three Fates: Clotho, who spun the thread of life, Lachesis, who measured it out, and Atropos, who cut it.

2.   The Greek mythological sea-goddess Tethys is not to be confused with Thetis, a later sea-divinity and mother of Achilles. The confusion is especially common in French, where the two names are homonyms.

3.   I am assuming, from La Fontaine's context, that both meanings of the English "spinster" are applicable to his characters.

The Satyr and the Passerby

1.   It probably bears mention that La Fontaine's satyr, his many offspring notwithstanding, is the mythological creature of that name—half-man, half-goat—rather than simply an oversexed male.

ILLUST: Some references are conscious, others not, and I see them only after the fact. I thought I was inventing a vulgar passerby, but having just used Dürer as a reference for "Dame Fortune amd the Child," Dürer must have been on my mind. Looking at this figure now, I see a more than passing resemblance to Ulrich Varnbuller, the subject of Dürer's large woodcut portrait of 1500. D.S.

The Horse and the Wolf

ILLUST: The fable "The Fox, the Wolf, and the Horse" from *Fifty More Fables of La Fontaine* (Urbana: University of Illinois Press, 1998), while different in story and moral, contains an image so similar—a wolf examining the hoof of a horse, which I had already drawn—that I couldn't initially revisualize it:

Searching about for a new version of the same subject, I saw a T'ang dynasty ceramic horse and my father's old stethoscope, resulting in an illustration that is more reflective of the flotsam and jetsam of my studio than of La Fontaine's text. D.S.

Dame Fortune and the Child

ILLUST: The figure of Dame Fortune comes directly from the large engraving *Nemesis (Great Fortune)* of 1500 by Albrecht Dürer. While Dürer shows her standing balanced on a crystal globe (as she glides above the world), French artists usually depict her standing on a wheel, so I adopted that conceit. Dürer clearly knew the epigram "Grab Fortune by the forelock, for she is bald behind!" and I have taken this coiffure and updated it to current punk/hip-hop fashion, which suggested appropriate piercings. D.S.

The Hare and the Partridge

1. Two of the three dogs' names used by La Fontaine here and in the following lines are discussed in detail by Regnier (*Op. cit.*, 1, 278; 417–18), who indicates that they imply the nicknames I have given the animals (even if the poet doesn't). While the third, Rustaut, goes unexplained—though there would seem to be at least a suggestion of "rusticity" in it—I take the liberty of characterizing him as "the Wise," given La Fontaine's (sarcastic?) assurance of his infallibility as one *"qui n'a jamais menti"* ("who has never told a lie").

The Eagle and the Owl

1. Given the scenario, I take the logical liberty of making La Fontaine's owl a female, despite the masculine gender of the noun *hibou*. I also take the artistic liberty of not reproducing in translation the most unusual—in fact, unique—quintuple rhyme of the original

here. Not especially felicitous in French, it would, I think be even less so in English.

2.   The name Megæra (see p. 31, note 2) has long been used in French to allude to a shrewish female, as in *La Mégère apprivoisée*, the usual French translation of Shakespeare's *The Taming of the Shrew*.

3.   I hardly need call to the reader's attention that my gratuitous pun does not exist in the original.

The Shepherd and the Lion

1.   Some might be tempted to see here a bit of tongue-in-cheek self-ridicule. While no one would accuse his characteristic digressions of being mere "empty ornament," it is hard to take seriously La Fontaine's seeming defense of concision.

2.   In a note of his own La Fontaine explains that the "certain Greek" in question was "Gabrias." It was by that deformed name that early centuries, La Fontaine's included, knew some of the quatrains of the 3rd-century Greek (or Hellenized Roman) poet Babrius (or Babrios, or Babrias), whose work was not more definitively brought to light until the 1840s. For illuminating details, see Regnier's note to the present fable (*Op. cit.*, VI, 3).

Phœbus and Boreas

1.   Unlike others who had treated—and would treat—this celebrated subject of worldwide folkloric diffusion, La Fontaine chooses to use the mythological names of his characters. (See, for example, the version by 16th-century fabulist Philibert Guide, a.k.a. "Hégémon," in my volume, *The Fabulists French: Verse Fables of Nine Centuries* [Urbana: University of Illinois Press, 1992], p. 27.)

The Wagoner Stuck in the Mud

1.   The town of Quimpercorentin (or Quimper-Corentin, in some editions) was the county seat of a district in Brittany. La Fontaine's opprobrium, more than the result of mere anti-provincial prejudice, would seem to have been shared by many. (See Regnier, *Op. cit.*, II, 58–59.)

2.   As Regnier points out (*Op. cit.*, II, 60), the reference to Hercules is slightly askew, since the god was asked by Atlas to replace him briefly in holding up the heavens, not the earth. But La Fontaine's mythological intent is clear.

3.   Again, the poet's punctuational imprecision lets the reader of the French guess whether his moral—one of many to become proverbial—is pronounced by Hercules or by La Fontaine himself. For another example in the present collection see "The Hare and the Frogs" (p. 27).

The Charlatan

1. The Acheron, "River of Sorrows," was one of the five rivers of the underworld in Greek mythology. (I invoke translator's license here to allude instead to the better-known Styx.) La Fontaine's reference suggests the death-defying tricks common to the outdoor magicians and quack-healers of the time, no less than to the illusionists of our own.

2. Less elegant a coinage than La Fontaine's *passe-Cicéron* ("Cicero-surpasser"), mine attempts to echo at least his meaning and his effect.

3. As Regnier observes (*Op. cit.*, II, 64–66), the *soutane* ("cassock") of the original was not exclusively a priestly garment in the 17th century, as it is today, but was also used, as implied here, by lay clerics and academics.

4. Arcadian mounts, both horses and asses, were, according to Regnier, famous through antiquity. (See *Op. cit.*, I, 65.)

5. Though *la Mort* ("Death") is personified in French as feminine, because of the grammatical gender of the noun, I opt here for the masculine pronoun, usual in English when referring to the Grim Reaper.

The Wishes

1. Readers interested in the probable source of this tale, from the Hebrew (and eventually, Indian) *Parables of Sendebar*, will find it extensively discussed in the Regnier edition (*Op. cit.*, II, 119–22).

2. This fable is designated as number 6 of Book VII in those collections where a pair of preceding fables, "Le Héron" and "La Fille" (not translated here), are presented each with a separate number rather than in tandem. (The disparity is, of course, continued thoughout the succeeding fables of the same book.)

King Lion's Court

1. Regnier (*Op. cit.*, II, 130-31) devotes a lengthy and informative note to the trained monkey known as Fagotin, who performed outside the theater of a popular marionettist, Brioché, during the mid-17th century. There is some question as to whether the name may have, in fact, been used by more than one performer.

2. Though La Fontaine's use of three consecutive lines with the same rhyme is occasionally met with—in this volume see, as the first instance, "The Lark, Her Little Ones, and the Farmer Who Owns the Field" (p. 70, lines 1–3)—the present example ("...*irrité*, ...*dégouté*, ...*severité*") is most unusual in that the line following (*Et, flateur*

excessif, il loüa la colère) has no rhyme at all, clearly a rare and inexplicable oversight on La Fontaine's part, but one that gives heart to translators, who are, themselves, human also. (I have been careful not to let my humanity show through here, and have avoided reproducing La Fontaine's error.) The present *lapsus calami* is discussed in detail by Regnier (*Op. cit.*, II, 131–32.)

3. The French expression *répondre en Normand* attributes to the Normans, known for their shrewdness, the special art of evasive reply.

The Man Who Runs After Fortune, and the Man Who Waits for Her in His Bed

1. La Fontaine's allusion to a cabbage-planter-turned-pope is rather obscure, according to Regnier (*Op. cit.*, II, 162), whose characteristically thorough research would certainly have explained it if anyone's could.

2. My high school English teacher, Julius Finn—a gentleman and a gentle man— would be pleased to see that, years after he had tried to convince me of the utility of the shall/will distinction, exigencies of rhyme have convinced me that he was right.

3. The reference is to the pompous ceremonial *levers* ("arisings") and *couchers* ("retirings") of Louis XIV, attended by favored members of the royal household and assorted dignitaries. The protocol of these events is explained in detail in *La Grande Encyclopédie*, 31 vols. (Paris: La Société Anonyme de la Grande Encyclopédie, *et al.*, 1886-1902), XIII, 29–30; XXII, 135.

4. Surat, north of Bombay, had been the first English foothold in India, since 1612, and eventually became one of the richest and most trafficked commercial centers in the Orient, visited especially by pilgrims to Mecca.

5. See p. 121, note 2.

ILLUST. The city to which the man who runs after fortune looks is an homage to Maxfield Parrish. It is a reworking of the architecture in an illustration that has always been a particular favorite of mine because it touches the geography of my life. A bearded artist standing in front of a walled domed city looks down at a boy and asks "You haven't been to Rome, have you?" from *The Golden Age* by Kenneth Grahame (London and New York: John Lane: The Bodley Head, 1900). If this architecture seems to have a more immediate familiarity, it is because it is copied in the latest installment of *Star Wars*. D.S.

The Cat, the Weasel, and the Little Rabbit

1.   La Fontaine borrows the name for his venal cat cum judge from Rabelais (*Pantagruel*, Book III, chapter 21), and the name Grippeminaud, below, from the same author's work (Book V, chapters 11–15), in which the *chat fourré* ("fur-bedecked cat") is taken as emblematic of the hypocritical and pompous legal profession of the day. (For a wealth of detail see Regnier, *Op. cit.*, II, 187–91.)

The Cobbler and the Financier

1.   La Fontaine is apparently alluding to the Seven Sages of Greece—Solon of Athens, Chilo of Sparta, Thales of Miletos, Bias of Priene, Cleobulos of Lindos, Pittacos of Mitylene, an Periander of Corinth—although I don't know what specific classical text, if any, suggests that their varied wisdom brought them much happiness.

ILLUST. The figure of the cobbler is based on photographs of various bass-baritones (among them my cousin Frederich Schorr) in the role of Hans Sachs, possibly Wagner's most lovable character, from the opera *Die Meistersinger von Nürnberg*. D.S.

Women and Secrets

1.   French grammar being what it is, La Fontaine's title can be understood in either a general or specific sense. I think it is safe to assume that he intended the former.

ILLUST: My inspirations, if not my source, for this illustration were a *Saturday Evening Post* cover, (March 6, 1948) by Norman Rockwell, and a montage sequence in *The Women* by George Cukor (1939). D.S.

The Rat and the Oyster

1.   See p. 79, note 2.

2.   I take the liberty (translator's license?) of attributing to the rat this reflection that La Fontaine omits; one that, under the circumstances, seems warranted.

3.   Many La Fontaine morals with a proverbial ring to them were, in fact, like this one, introduced by him into the language. Others, while predating his use, no doubt owe much of their currency to their appearance in the *Fables*.

ILLUST. The characters in this fable allowed me to pay homage simultaneously not only to two of my favorite illustrators, John Tenniel and Ernest H. Shepard, but specifically to particularly loved images. The oysters (with feet!) are borrowed from Tenniel's illustration for Tweedledee's recitation of "The Walrus and the Carpenter" in *Through the Looking Glass,* by Lewis Carroll; the wayfarer, based on the Sea Rat in chapter 9, "Wayfarers All," of *The Wind in the Willows*, by Kenneth Grahame (London: Methuen & Company, 1931). D.S.

The Ass and the Dog

1.   See p. 117, note 4.

The Two Dogs and the Dead Ass

1.   This fable is an excellent example of La Fontaine's almost improvisational development of a subject. The opening lines point us in one direction, only to lead us, finally to an utterly unexpected moral conclusion.

The Oyster and the Adversaries

1.   I take the liberty of changing the peasant's name here to one more common to Anglophone ears and more readily pronounceable by Anglophone tongues. Suffice it to remind the reader that both "Perrin" and "Dandin" are traditional names for typically naïve rustics—ironic, under the circumstances, given this one's finesse—the latter immortalized in Molière's comedy *Georges Dandin.*

2.   Although the archaic expression *sac et quilles* has come to mean, roughly, "bag and baggage," La Fontaine is no doubt using it more literally in this less-than-limpid allusion. My rather free translation reflects (with considerable liberty) a reading offered by Regnier (*Op. cit.*, ii, 406).

The Wolf and the Scrawny Dog

1.   The earlier fable alluded to is "The Little Fish and the Fisherman" (v, 3). For my translation see *Fifty Fables of La Fontaine* (Urbana: University of Illinois Press, 1988), pp. 54–55.

All in Moderation

1.   See p. 69, note 1.

The Fishes and the Cormorant

1.   Given La Fontaine's scenario, his inclusion here of the wolf, and his exclusion of the bird, seem a little illogical. Without meaning to second-guess him, I have compromised by mentioning both animals in my version.

ILLUST. This *nature morte* of fish skeletons is an homage to the painter Hyman Bloom.

The Spider and the Swallow

1. I resist the temptation of making La Fontaine's reference more consistent by changing his Greek "Pallas"—she who sprang fully armed from Zeus's forehead—to the Latin "Minerva," in keeping with his use of "Jupiter." The enmity referred to is related in Ovid's *Metamorphoses* (Book VI, 1–145), where the young woman Arachne, expert in embroidery, was transformed into a spider after killing herself in despair over the wrath of Minerva, her rival in the art. As for the allusions to Progne (or Procne) and, below, Philomela, see the fable "Philomela and Procne" (pp. 34–35).

The Fishes and the Shepherd Who Plays the Flute

1. La Fontaine chooses the traditional pastoral name Tircis for his hero, and—his title inexplicably to the contrary—has him playing a likewise traditional *musette* ("bagpipe"). I follow him in this curious contradiction.

ILLUST: Just to confuse things further I show him playing a cross between a baroque recorder and a *cor anglais!* D.S.

2. My pun on the verb "to serve" is not wholly gratuitous, the French *traiter* suggesting, at least obliquely, a culinary meaning.

The Dream of the Man from Mogol Land

1. La Fontaine, certainly sophisticated enough not to confuse Mogol with Greco-Roman theology of the afterlife, is no doubt using the "Elysian Fields" here as a very general, non-specific reference.

2. This apparent acceptance of the notion that the stars influence human life is curious in light of La Fontaine's outspoken mockery of astrology in the fable "The Astrologer Who Happens to Fall into a Well" (see pp. 22–25). Even his great admirer, the 18th-century moralist Chamfort, called attention to the contradiction. (See Regnier, *Op. cit.*, III, 119–20.)

3. I take the liberty of specifying the Parque ("Fate") referred to in La Fontaine's allusion, since, from the context, it is clear that he is speaking of Clotho, the member of the trio who did the actual spinning of the thread of life. (See p. 79, note 1.)

ILLUST: After finishing this illustration, I found it troublingly familiar. Albeit unconscious, the source must certainly be Aubrey Beardsley's cover for *Ali Baba*. D.S.

The Wolf and the Fox

1.   As Ovid recounts in the *Metamorphoses* (Book I, 588ff.), Io, daughter of Inachos, first king of Argos, was turned into a heifer by Jupiter—who had, not uncharacteristically, taken a fancy to her—in order to save her from the jealous wrath of Juno.

The Mice and the Screech Owl

1.   See p. 79, note 1.

2.   The lengthy "Discours à Madame de la Sablière," inserted at the end of Book IX, contains La Fontaine's celebrated attempt to refute the Cartesian assumption that animals are mere machines. For him, while they may lack souls, they clearly are not unthinking automata.

3.   Like the prose passage between the fables "Death and the Wretched Man" and "Death and the Woodsman" (see p. 7), La Fontaine appends this explanation to his fable, and I keep it in the position to which he himself assigned it, rather than relegating it to a note. As for his perhaps naïve assurance of veracity, there is, to be sure, considerable question. (See Regnier, *Op. cit.*, III, 161.)

The Treasure-Hoarder and the Ape

1.   Bertrand, with and without the honorific "Dom" appended, is one of the two common names La Fontaine uses for his several simians, the other being Gille. For the fable in which he uses both, see "The Ape and the Leopard" in my collection *Fifty More Fables of La Fontaine* (Urbana: University of Illinois Press, 1998), pp. 104–07.

ILLUST: My source for the image of the ape counting money is a shot at the end of the train-wreck sequence in the film *The Greatest Show on Earth* (Cecil B. de Mille: 1952). D.S.

The Eagle and the Magpie

ILLUST: So as not to repeat the classic profile of the bald or golden eagle used in "The Owl and the Eagle" (p. 95), I turned to a more exotic source: the crested monkey-eating eagle of the Phillipines, an endangered species. If you think this doesn't look like an eagle I would tell you a favorite story of my father's. An Austrian aristocrat is out hunting. Shooting down a large bird, his gamekeeper runs ahead. Reaching the kill, he exclaims, "Sire, you've shot down an eagle." The lord catches up and looks down. "Dumkopf!" he says, chewing out the servant, "any idiot knows an eagle has two heads!" This graceful magpie, by the bye, is lifted directly from Audubon, whose beautiful drawing portrays the iridescence of the black feathers of this graphically handsome bird. D.S.

The Ape

1. One wants to believe, certainly, that La Fontaine's condemnation of plagiarists as worse even than wife-beaters is the pointed, very sardonic exaggeration of a man of letters. Be that as it may, I choose this fable to end my collection—fittingly, I think—with the ironic realization that translators, after all, are plagiarists too, in a sense, albeit self-confessed and (generally) harmless.

ILLUST: The concept for these illustrations—proceeding from the specific events in one Paris attic into the general population (of writers)—comes from Franco Zeffirelli's production of *La Bohème* for the Metropolitan Opera. In Act I we see a small cut-away garrett where the action takes place surrounded by the vast empty space of the stage. When we return to that same garret in Act IV, that space has filled in with the mansard rooftops of Paris, implying that a drama is playing out in each of them. D.S.

Bibliography

For the vast bibliography of secondary works relating to La Fontaine, I mention here, as in my previous volumes, only those book-length studies in English:

Jean Dominique Biard, *The Style of La Fontaine's "Fables"* (Oxford: Blackwell, 1966).

Anne L. Birberick, ed., *Refiguring La Fontaine: Tercentenary Essays* (Charlottesville, Va.: Rockwood Press, 1966).

Richard Danner, *Patterns of Irony in the "Fables" of La Fontaine* (Athens: Ohio University Press, 1985).

Margaret Guiton, *La Fontaine, Poet and Counterpoet* (New Brunswick, N.J.: Rutgers University Press, 1961).

Frank Hamel, *Jean de La Fontaine* (London: Stanley Paul, 1911; rpt., Port Washington, N.Y.: Kennikat Press, 1970).

Ethel M. King, *Jean de La Fontaine* (Brooklyn: Gaus, 1970).

Agnes Ethel Mackey, *La Fontaine and His Friends* (New York: Braziller, 1973).

David Lee Rubin, *A Pact with Silence: Art and Thought in the Fables of Jean de La Fontaine* (Columbus: Ohio State University Press, 1991).

Monica Sutherland, *La Fontaine* (London: Jonathan Cape, 1953; rpt., London: Jonathan Cape, 1974).

Marie-Odile Sweetser, *La Fontaine* (Boston: Twayne, 1987).

Michael Vincent, *Figures of the Text: Reading and Writing in La Fontaine* (Amsterdam and Philadelphia: John Benjamin, 1992).

Philip Wadsworth, *Young La Fontaine* (Evanston, Ill.: Northwestern University Press, 1952).

The following, while devoted primarily to La Fontaine's less generally well-known *Contes* (1665–74), contains stylistic observations applicable as well to his *Fables:*

John Clarke Lapp, *The Esthetics of Negligence: La Fontaine's "Contes"* (Cambridge: Cambridge University Press, 1971).

of SCHORR 'TIS SAID THAT NO TRANSLATOR
COULD FIND A WITTIER ILLUSTRATOR!

AVE, JOHN HOLLANDER, ALL HAIL!
SCHOLAR AND POET, PRIDE OF YALE

NE WOULD, HIMSELF REJOICE
HIS VERSE IN SILLS' FINE VOICE

Oh! the translator's lot obtuse
He must traduire yet not traduce

Compact Disc

vocal: **Douglas Sills**

direction: Judy Weinstein

1. The Ploughman and His Sons
2. The Sheperd and the Lion & The Lion and the Hunter
3. The Drunkard and His Wife
4. Phœbus and Boreas
5. The Hare and the Frogs
6. The Eagle and the Magpie
7. Death and the Wretched Man & Death and the Woodsman
8. The Wolf and the Scrawny Dog
9. The Lark, Her Little Ones, and the Farmer Who Owns the Field
10. The Wolves and the Ewes
11. The Wagoner Stuck in the Mud
12. The Rats in Council Assembled
13. The Fishes and the Cormorant
14. The Charlatan
15. The Oracle and the Infidel
16. The Sheperd and the Sea
17. The Gardener and His Lord
18. The Horse and the Wolf
19. The Spider and the Swallow
20. The Wolf and the Fox
21. The Ass and the Pup
22. The Horse Who Sought Revenge on the Stag
23. The Hornets and the Honeybees
24. The Hare and the Partridge
25. The Cobbler and the Financier
26. All in Moderation

recorded at PhotoMag, New York City
courtesy: Arthur Williams & Mark Polyocon
sound engineer: Douglas Senger